The Quarriers Story

William Quarrier

The Quarriers Story

A History of Quarriers

Anna Magnusson

BIRLINN

In association with
Quarriers Homes
Bridge of Weir, Scotland

This revised edition published in 2006 by
Birlinn Limited
West Newington House
10 Newington Road
Edinburgh
EH9 1QS
UK

www.birlinn.co.uk

First published in 1984 by Quarriers Homes,
Bridge of Weir, Scotland
Copyright © Anna Magnusson 1984, 2006

ISBN10: 1 84158 494 0
ISBN13: 978 1 84158 494 2

British Library Cataloguing-in-Publication Data
A catalogue record for this book is available from the British Library

Typeset by Wordsense, Edinburgh
Printed and bound by GraphyCems, Spain

Acknowledgements

It's more than twenty years since *The Village* was first published and in that time Quarriers has radically changed. A revision and updating of the story was called for, and here it is. *The Quarriers Story* tries to cover the main developments which have taken place over the past two decades – and are still taking place – and to continue where *The Village* left off. I have changed the title to reflect one of the biggest differences between the Quarriers of today and the Quarriers of twenty years ago: the organisation's main work now takes place far beyond the boundaries of the Village at Bridge of Weir. It has moved to cities and communities all over Scotland.

To all the people who gave me their time, energies and expertise when I began the mammoth task of writing the original book, I say a sincere thank you once again. Many are no longer with Quarriers. The impetus for this revision has come from Quarriers itself and I am indebted to the Chief Executive Phil Robinson for his patience and willingness to talk about both the positive and negative aspects of the organisation he leads. The other person who has been unfailing in his enthusiasm for an updating of the story is Fred Wardle of the Quarriers Canadian Family, and I would like to thank him and his wife Susan for all their help. The Canadian part of the Quarriers story has been substantially expanded for this book, and I could not have done this without the reflections and experiences of Quarriers emigrants and their families, so honestly and vividly shared with me.

To them, and to the many, many former Quarriers boys and girls all over Britain who have contributed their memories of Quarriers, both happy and sad, I say, simply, thank you. At its heart, *The Quarriers Story* is all about their stories.

Anna Magnusson
March 2006

Illustrations

page 14 taken from Swan's *Beauties of the Clyde* (Greenock Central Library)

pages 19, 22, 29 and 30 taken from Annan's *Closes of Glasgow, 1868–1877* (The Mitchell Library)

page 88 taken from Barnardo Photographic Archive

page 91 taken from *The Home Children*, published by Watson & Dwyer Publishing Ltd, and reproduced by kind permission from the Public Archives Canada/PA-117285

All other sources for illustrations are given in the captions. Uncredited illustrations are copyright and are reproduced courtesy of Quarriers Homes.

Contents

For Mum, Dad and Anna

Foreword

It all began with a man possessed: possessed by a sublime idea, an ardent passion, a blazing desire to help deprived and hapless children in Glasgow. His name was William Quarrier.

This book is the story of that man and his idea. It tells how that idea became reality in a beautiful rural corner of Renfrewshire as a 'Children's City', at Bridge of Weir. This infant Village, founded in 1878, was dedicated to the task of rescuing abandoned and orphaned children from the teeming squalor of Glasgow's back streets and giving them a new life. But, like time itself, the idea did not stand still, and this book vividly chronicles its evolution into a modern voluntary care organisation – the third largest in Scotland – which runs more than eighty projects across the country.

This is *The Quarriers Story*.

William Quarrier (1829–1903) was an archetypal product of the Victorian Age: born in Greenock and brought up in Glasgow in grinding poverty, fostered on religion and nourished by the Victorian ideals of self-help and pride in status. But in Quarrier's case, the Victorian sense of rectitude never ossified into self-righteousness; he never preached what he didn't practise. After he had 'made good' as a businessman in Glasgow, pulling himself up by the boot-straps to start a chain of shoe shops, his own success never blinded him to the desperate needs of others, and with evangelical fervour he started a revolution in social attitudes towards the underprivileged – a continuing revolution to which he devoted all the rest of his life and which today encompasses the world.

In this modern age of vast social work departments and childcare schemes, it isn't easy to imagine the horrors of a deprived childhood in industrial cities more than a century ago; nor is it easy to conceive of the courage, the audacity even, of William Quarrier's enterprise, his single-minded determination to give homeless children, for the first time in their short lives, a home.

Ah, but what is a home? The Victorians tended to sentimentalise the idea of home, just as they tended to romanticise the idea of childhood itself. Home, Sweet Home! Home is where the heart is! What is home without a mother? As John Masefield was to write in a celebrated passage in his poem *The Everlasting Mercy*:

> And he who gives a child a treat
> Makes joy-bells ring in Heaven's street,
> And he who gives a child a home
> Builds palaces in Kingdom come.

It took a man like William Quarrier to make a 'home' a practical reality for thousands of homeless children. Quarrier wanted to get away from the institutional care of children, the vast impersonal halls and dormitories of the poorhouse; instead he conceived, built and personally ran a growing complex of cottages homes at Bridge of Weir, with house-mothers and house-fathers in charge of small groups of children: families, not inmates.

Not content with that, he plunged energetically into pioneering emigration schemes designed to give 'his' children a new life and a new future in the New World, in Canada. He pioneered free sanatoria at Bridge of Weir for the treatment of that terrible scourge of yesteryear, tuberculosis. He built a Colony for the treatment of people with epilepsy, which offered sanctuary to the victims of the 'falling disease' long before it was properly understood – and all in a spirit of what he himself described as 'sanctified common sense'.

Over the decades since Quarrier built his Children's City at Bridge of Weir there have been many changes, of course, to keep abreast with the changing times – especially in the sixty years since the Second World War. The cottage-groups became too large. Sometimes discipline became excessive, even cruel. Brothers and sisters were separated and segregated. The Canadian emigration scheme suffered when examples of gross exploitation and neglect of British children came to light. These were bitter blots on a magnificent record; but they were also milestones in the growth of public acceptance of the need for communal, social responsibility for all the helpless in our midst. More than a century after the foundation of Quarrier's Homes there have been many revolutions in ideas about child welfare: children's Homes (with a capital H) have been shut down all over the place; fostering, family centres and helping children in their own communities have, for many years, been the order of the day, and even the best of the old traditional Homes are now regarded as totally obsolete.

The men and women who have carried on Quarrier's work down the years have always been strong on tradition; but they have never been afraid of change. In tune with changing demand in the 1980s, when the need for traditional Children's Homes decreased rapidly, Quarrier's Homes transformed itself from a 'Children's City' into a wider caring community. The unique Village at Bridge of Weir now cares for needy groups of all kinds, both young and old, able and disabled – a village which provides sheltered accommodation for the elderly, respite care for children with learning difficulties and supported living for people with epilepsy. Some schemes are run in cooperation with the local authority, others by charitable organisations using the fine facilities provided by Quarriers.

During the 1990s and the early years of the twenty-first century, that vision was superseded by a more outward-looking philosophy, which has taken William Quarrier's commitment to caring far beyond the geographical boundaries of the Village at Bridge of Weir. His original idea has burgeoned almost unrecognisably into areas of need which are very different now from what they were in Victorian Scotland; but its essential spirit has never changed.

These are fine achievements, to be trumpeted and celebrated. But the author does not attempt to fudge the failures, any more than Quarriers has done – in particular, the sickening cases of child abuse at the Village in the 1960s, which have come to light only in recent years.

The Quarriers Story tells the whole tale of the passing years, of these changing times – and of the thousands of lives which were transformed.

It is much more than a deserved tribute to William Quarrier and to the men and women of Quarriers down the years. It is a story of high hope and heroism, of determination and dedication, of warmth and willingness, of conscience and compassion.

It is a never-ending story which lifts the heart.

Magnus Magnusson
March 2006

Chapter 1

Beginnings

It all began more than 150 years ago in a small street within sight and sound of the docks of Greenock. It was there, in a close off Cross Shore Street – a narrow lane running down the quayside where lighters loaded their cargo, and steamboats from Glasgow disgorged their passengers – that William Quarrier was born on 29 September 1829.

Greenock, on Scotland's Firth of Clyde, was in 1829 a busy industrial town with an illustrious shipbuilding history. Scott's Shipbuilding and Engineering Company of Greenock, founded in 1711, was one of the many companies which helped to make Greenock the centre of shipbuilding on the Clyde during the eighteenth century. By the early nineteenth century new shipbuilding centres had developed further up the Clyde, notably at Port Glasgow and Dumbarton, but Greenock was still the chief highway to the Atlantic, and every day great ocean-going liners anchored out at the Tail o' the Bank. Greenock could also claim fame as the birthplace of James Watt, inventor of the steam engine. And now, ten years after Watt's death, another child destined for fame was born.

William Quarrier was the second of three children, and had an older and a younger sister. The family had little money and his mother often had to look after the household on her own for long periods while her husband plied his trade as a ship's carpenter, calling at ports all over the world. It was while William's father was working on a ship in Quebec that disaster struck: he contracted cholera and died, leaving his family

Customs House Quay, Greenock (reproduced by courtesy of Greenock Central Library)

destitute thousands of miles away across the sea. Annie Quarrier had three children to feed and clothe, and no source of income, so she had to try to provide by herself. She opened a small shop in Greenock but it was not successful and, after months of worry and despair, trying

Broomielaw in Quarrier's day (reproduced by courtesy of The Mitchell Library)

to make ends meet, she decided that she would have to move the family to Glasgow and find work there. She scraped together enough for the fares for one of the big steamers which ran daily between Greenock and Glasgow and, one afternoon in 1834, William Quarrier, just five years old, stood with his family on Glasgow's busy Broomielaw quayside where all the big Clyde steamers docked.

Early Victorian Glasgow was in the throes of industrial expansion. The city was superbly placed for trade with the world: down the Clyde lay the route to the Atlantic and commerce with the American continent; to the east, the Forth and Clyde Canal opened the way to the North Sea and Europe. All along the Broomielaw, great ships, heavy with cargo, lined the docks five or six deep, waiting to unload their goods and materials from all over the world – timber from South American forests, sugar and rum from the West Indies, fish and chemicals from Europe and Russia. Passenger and cargo steamboats nudged past one another on their way to Liverpool, Belfast and Dublin, and as they went bustling down the river they would meet vessels heading for Glasgow from local resorts all over the Firth, such as Millport on the Isle of Cumbrae and Rothesay on the Isle of Bute.

William Quarrier's birthplace in Cross Shore Street, Greenock

The city's famous Tobacco Lords, once to be seen strolling along the Trongate in their scarlet cloaks, were gone now and in their footsteps walked men whose money lay in Glasgow's new booming industry – cotton: tons and tons of it, pouring into the city for delivery to Scotland's 134 mills, almost all of them within twenty-five miles of Glasgow. The cotton and textiles industry spawned a host of factories all over the city, employing thousands of men, women and children. Dotted thickly on both sides of the river were spinning and weaving mills, lawn and cambric manufacturers, linen printers and dyers, sewed muslin makers, yarn merchants, chemical and dye works, steam-engine manufacturers. Glasgow also boasted other industries besides cotton; many people worked in the iron, brick and glass works and, in a little village called Govan on the south bank of the river, were the beginnings

The stone archway to Quarrier's birthplace in Cross Shore Street now forms the War Memorial just inside the main entrance to the Village

of marine engineering which was to be the cornerstone of the city's industry from the 1860s onwards.

It was to this expanding, wealthy city that the Quarrier family came to make a new start. But, with very little money, they were forced to live in one of the poorest and most overcrowded areas of the city. Like thousands of others, they experienced the dark side of Glasgow's industrial success and joined the ranks of the city's growing population of poor, crowded in dark and dingy tenements amid factory and mill.

With the expansion of industry and the vast migration of people from rural areas to the city in search of jobs, among them a constant stream of Irish, Glasgow's population had rocketed from 42,832 in 1780 to 110,460 in 1811 and more than 200,000 at the beginning of the 1830s. This caused severe overcrowding in certain parts of the city with which the authorities simply could not cope. At that time Glasgow was divided into four completely separate and independent burghs, and there was no one single authority responsible for clearing the overcrowded areas and building better houses. The worst spot was the rectangle of alleys and wynds formed by the Trongate to the north, the Saltmarket and Stockwell Street to the east and west, and the riverside to the south. Time and again since the early years of the century this area had been singled out as a black spot containing the worst elements of appalling housing, insanitary conditions and disease-ridden streets. One particularly strong critic was a Mr J.C. Symons, a government official who was sent to Glasgow in 1835 to inspect the living conditions of handloom weavers across the river in Paisley. Mr Symons was so appalled by some of the places he saw in the centre of Glasgow that he could not refrain from including in his report a vivid description of the horrors he encountered:

> The Wynds of Glasgow comprise a fluctuating population of from 15,000 to 20,000 persons. This quarter consists of a labyrinth of lanes, out of which numberless entrances lead into small courts, each with a reeking dunghill in the centre. Revolting as was the outside appearance of these places, I was little prepared for the filth and destitution within. In some of these lodging-houses (visited at night) we found a whole lair of human beings littered along the floor, sometimes fifteen or twenty, some clothed and some naked, men, women and children, huddled promiscuously together. Their bed consisted of a layer of musty straw intermixed with rags. There was generally no furniture in these places.

It was in a close off the teeming High Street, on the edge of this most congested area of the city, that the Quarriers found a room. The High Street, notorious for the length and narrowness of its closes, was one of the four main streets which formed the ancient centre of Glasgow. The Saltmarket, the Trongate, High Street and the Gallowgate all converged at Glasgow Cross. These streets had been the business hub of eighteenth-century Glasgow, but by the time the Quarriers arrived the middle-classes had long ago migrated to the west of the city, leaving their once-elegant two- and three-storey apartments to house far more people than they were ever meant for.

In their High Street room Annie Quarrier tried to provide for the family by taking in fine sewing from one of the big warehouses. William

A typical Glasgow close: No. 118 High Street
(reproduced by courtesy of The Mitchell Library)

helped her by carrying the finished bundles back to the warehouse and collecting more, but there was never enough work for his mother to make ends meet. So, at the age of seven, William was sent to work in a factory (probably the one owned by George Stewart, Pin Maker and Wire Drawer) in Graeme Street, near the Gallowgate. For ten or twelve hours a day, six days a week, he sat at a table and fixed the ornamental head tops on to pins – and all for the princely sum of one shilling a week. It was not in the least unusual for a child of his age to work those sorts of hours. Before the 1833 Factory Act to 'Regulate the Labour of Children and Young Persons in Mills and Factories', the normal working day for children from six years upwards in the cotton mills was anything between nine and twelve hours. Young boys and girls were employed as 'scavengers', crawling under the machines to pick up fluff and rubbish, or as 'piecers' whose job was to tie the threads together when they broke. Down in the coalmines, children spent long, damp, dark hours crouched beside the little doors which they had to open when the coal trolleys were sent along the line. In print works, lace factories and matchmaking factories young boys and girls worked alongside men and women, doing a full day's work for small reward. For hundreds of families like the Quarriers, sending the children out to work was the only way of surviving.

But even with William's contribution to the family's budget, the Quarriers were very, very poor. Years later he wrote of the hardships of these early days – in particular, he remembered one day when he stood in the High Street 'barefooted, bareheaded, cold and hungry, having tasted no food for a day and a half'. Poverty like that was common on the streets of Glasgow and many were much worse off than the Quarriers. At least William's family had his weekly shilling and whatever his mother earned, but for those with no source of income there was only parish relief. Since the sixteenth century, Scottish parishes had given small amounts of money to those who could prove that they were in need and unable to provide for themselves. The Kirk raised the money through voluntary collections, funeral dues and other such means, and this was then distributed among poor families in the parish. In Glasgow money was raised through compulsory assessment of the means of the wealthier members of the town and distributed under the auspices of the Town Hospital.

To be dependent upon poor relief in nineteenth-century Glasgow was to be among the lowest and most wretched in society. Paupers were looked down on by the hard-working respectable citizens, and the amount of money to which a person on poor relief was entitled was usually very little, enough only for a very spartan way of life – and sometimes not even for that; according to one Donald Ross, an agent of the Glasgow Association in Aid of the Poor, some paupers had to survive on appallingly little, barely enough for food and warmth. Ross compiled a document in 1847 entitled *Pictures of Pauperism: The condition of the poor described by themselves in fifty genuine letters, addressed by paupers to the agent of the Glasgow Association in Aid of the Poor*; in his indignant Preface to the letters, Ross cites the example of an old widow who lived in a tiny apartment. She was:

> …without food, without proper clothing, without fuel, and without furniture. She was allowed five shillings per month by the parish, out of which she paid three shillings per month for rent, leaving two shillings a month, or *little more than three farthings a day for food, fuel and clothing!*

According to Ross, such low payments were by no means unusual.

Another feature of the workings of the Poor Law in Scotland was that, traditionally, poor relief could only be administered to those who were destitute and *disabled;* in other words, if a man were unemployed but able-bodied he was not officially entitled to parish aid. He might be given a little money in return for some sort of community work – breaking stones on the highway, for instance – or the Poor Inspector might tide him over with something for a day or two, but officially only widows, sick or infirm men, deserted wives, orphans, deserted children and the aged were eligible for relief. This meant great hardship during the periods of mass unemployment, such as the 'Hungry Forties', but it stemmed from a widespread attitude that unemployment was somehow the fault of the individual, and that a man without a job simply hadn't looked hard enough for one.

Those not entitled to poor relief had to turn to one of the many charitable organisations and voluntary societies, such as the Glasgow Society for Benevolent Visitation of the Destitute Sick and Others in Extreme Poverty, a high-falutin' title for a very practical society which issued tickets entitling the holder to food, clothing and other necessities

The High Street, Glasgow (reproduced by courtesy of The Mitchell Library)

at certain specified shops all over the city. *The New Statistical Account* for 1841 listed thirty-three 'Benevolent and Charitable Institutions of Glasgow, exclusive of Widows' Funds, Benefit Societies, Charity Schools and Maintenance of Paupers', and new societies were being formed all the time to try to ease the hardships of poverty and want suffered by so many.

The Quarriers bore their share of hunger and want as they eked out a living, day by day. But William's mother realised that he needed a proper trade to secure his own and the family's future, so when William was about eight years old she had him apprenticed to a shoemaker in the High Street. Most of his work consisted of running around after the men in the shop, lighting their pipes, fetching and carrying and preparing the rosined threads for sewing. This did not last for long, however; according to John Urquhart, Quarrier's earliest biographer, the business went bankrupt through the intemperate drinking habits of the owner. So another situation was found for William with a shoemaker in Paisley, on the south side of the River Clyde. This meant he had to walk there and back every day – a distance of some thirteen miles. And the shoemaker's apprentice didn't even have a pair of shoes of his own! But William Quarrier was a determined little character and one cold, dark New Year's Eve he even raced the stagecoach into the city on his way back from work. He doggedly chased it mile after mile, as the coach bumped through the gas-lit streets, and by the time it reached the 'Half-Way House' in Paisley Road West the passengers were so amazed and delighted by the tenacity of the skinny boy running behind that they started to throw him coins and cheer him on. They dragged William into the warm inn parlour and plied him with food and drink. Then, flushed with Hogmanay bonhomie and 'Half-Way House' beer, they ushered him into the coach and paid his fare the rest of the way to Glasgow.

It's a story too irresistibly true to the character of the man to be the mere invention of a devoted biographer. That boy became the young man who, years later, joined Blackfriars Church in Glasgow and, appalled at the poor attendance, determined to do something about it. With great deliberateness he chose an empty pew and week after week invited friends and acquaintances to accompany him to church until the pew was filled. Then he started on the pew behind and repeated the whole process. After a few months, Blackfriars Church was considerably busier than when William Quarrier had joined.

Young William worked hard at his trade and, at only twelve, became a journeyman shoemaker. It was a remarkably early age at which to have learned the trade, but such was his application and skill that he had no difficulty in keeping up with the older men in the shop. In the next four years he gained experience and perfected his trade by moving around Glasgow, working for short periods in various boot and shoe shops, until he found a situation with a Mrs Hunter, who owned premises in the elegant and fashionable Argyle Street.

By this time William was earning sufficient money to provide his family with better accommodation and he was able to rent a small house in Alston Street (where the Central Station now stands). Gradually he was pulling himself up from the grinding poverty of the early years.

During the years he worked for Mrs Hunter he was introduced by her to Blackfriars Street Baptist Church. There, at the age of seventeen, William first declared his Christian faith, a faith awesome in its simplicity and strength. Years later he wrote of his conversion in one of the annual accounts of his work:

> For the first time I heard the great truth of the Gospel, that 'God so loved the world that He gave His only begotten Son, that whosoever believeth in Him should not perish, but have everlasting life'. Under the influence of the Spirit and teaching of the Word of God, I was led to accept of Christ as all my salvation.

And that was it. No fuss, no momentous doubts and struggles to overcome, and yet a faith which was to be the life-long inspiration and motivation of all Quarrier's work among Scotland's poor and orphaned children.

The second great event of Quarrier's life for which Mrs Hunter could claim a share of the credit was his marriage to Isabella, Mrs Hunter's daughter. William courted her for ten years before they finally married in December 1856. By that time William Quarrier was a rising man. He had opened his first boot and shoemaker's shop, at the age of twenty-four, at 243 Argyle Street, and this proved so successful that he moved to larger premises further along the street in 1861. William Quarrier seemed set for a profitable future in business; indeed, in the next few years he was to open further boot-making shops in Glasgow, one in the Gallowgate in 1867 and another in Cowcaddens in 1869, which made him one of the city's first multiple store owners. But by that time he was also involved in work with the poor children of the city, work which made him no money and which would ultimately lead to his giving up the shoemaking business. It all resulted from an incident one winter's night in 1864.

Chapter 2

'Like Moses of Old'

It was a cold, raw night in November 1864, and William Quarrier was walking back home to Kingston Place after a long day's business in the city. As he turned into Jamaica Street and headed towards the Old Bridge he caught sight of a small figure in the shadows at the side of the street. It was a young boy, a match-seller. He was crying bitterly. Quarrier stopped to ask him what was wrong and, between sobs, the

Jamaica Bridge (reproduced by courtesy of The Mitchell Library)

lad told him that an older boy had just stolen all his stock and evening's earnings while his back was turned.

Quarrier comforted the boy and gave him enough money to replenish his matches, but as he continued on his way he could not put the incident out of his mind. For some years now, ever since he had started in business for himself and settled into a comfortable way of life, a conviction had been growing inside him, sharpened by his sense of Christian responsibility, that he could not remain all his life just a Glasgow businessman. Every day he saw the city's poor folk, the children on the street corners, day and night, selling newspapers and matches, families singing and begging for pennies – all a constant reminder of his own poor beginnings. He felt a duty to help, as he described years later in the first Annual Report he published on his work among children:

> Like Moses of old, I had a strong desire to go down to my brethren, the children of the streets, and endeavour to lead them from a life of misery and shame to one of usefulness and honour.

But he felt unfitted for such a great undertaking. Surely someone else would take up the work, someone with abundant means, time and talent? But that night in November, confronted by one of his 'brethren', Quarrier could put off his decision no longer: he was the one to do the work, and he would accept the challenge.

So he went home and wrote a letter which appeared in the *Glasgow Herald* on 2 December 1864:

> Sir,
> On my occasional visits to London I have been much pleased with many of the sights to be seen there, but with none more than with the tidy and clean appearance of the London Shoe-Black Brigade, an institution peculiar to London. There are to be seen many hundreds of youths who have none to care for them, fed, clothed and educated from their own earnings, in brushing boots and shoes, and sent forth into the world to be useful members of society. No doubt many of these youths, if left to themselves, would become wrecks on the great sea of London life, but as it is they are an honour to the nation for industry and perseverance, and these good results may be chiefly attributed to those gentlemen who give a little of their spare time to the management of the Society. Always on my return to Glasgow I have wished that we had such an institution here. I think we have need of it. In almost every street of our city are to be found youths who have none to care for

them and possessing all the elements of industry and perseverance. If these were formed into a Glasgow Shoe-Black Brigade the same results as have followed the London institution might be fairly looked for here. Now, sir, if a number of gentlemen would come forward (which I am sure many would be glad to do), I would be happy to be one of them, giving of my time and substance towards this object. I have no doubt, with the aid of your pen and that of your contemporaries, of the success of such an undertaking. Although it might not have an annual revenue of £40,000 like the Great Western Cooking Depot Scheme, yet if it fed, clothed and educated forty destitute youths, preserving them from the vices that surround them and making them useful members of society, I say that the result would far transcend any pecuniary aid that might be given to it.

Yours truly,

SHOEBLACK

The response to Quarrier's letter was not overwhelming. Some scoffed that it would never work, that it would be impossible to train street boys for a worthwhile occupation and, anyway, Glasgow was too rainy for a shoeblack to be able to do business. Nonsense, replied Quarrier; there were already many boys doing just that, but they needed to be organised, educated and looked after. His plan was that the boys would work as a part of a uniformed team, charging a ha'penny per shoeshine and giving a percentage of their earnings toward the cost of their stock and uniform, board and lodging if they needed it, and the night classes which Quarrier planned they should all attend.

Provost John Blackie, the head of the well-known Glasgow publishing firm, was one of the first to offer Quarrier his support. Gradually others followed and a committee was formed to plan the work. But Quarrier was not a committee man and had no patience with the deliberations and discussions which ensued. He itched to see his scheme in action and became so irritated at the slow way the matter was proceeding that James Pagan, the editor of the *Glasgow Herald*, remarked to him one day, 'Mr Quarrier, if this work is to be done, you will have to do it yourself'.

Quarrier did just that and forged ahead on his own. He began by scouring the stations and street corners where many shoeblacks were to be found and invited some forty of them to his house for tea to discuss his proposition. Most came, and were glad they had done so when they saw the spread of sandwiches and cakes which Mrs Quarrier had provided.

Quarrier wisely waited until they had eaten their fill before outlining his plan. The boys would work during the day and attend reading and writing classes in the evening and Sabbath School each week. At Sabbath School they would practise their reading by learning Scripture texts and reading from the Bible. A hundred years ago such Sabbath Schools were the only way that a great many children could learn to read and write, because they were working the other six days of the week. This was how Quarrier himself had acquired all his early education.

On the financial side, Quarrier explained to the boys that they would receive eight pence out of every shilling they earned. Each boy would be issued with a uniform – a cap and navy-blue flannel jacket trimmed with red, and a red badge on the arm. Every boy would be independent to work at his own pace and wherever he wanted, but would be responsible, too, as part of a team.

After the boys trooped out that evening (helping themselves to one or two little ornaments and valuable-looking objects on the way, as Mrs Quarrier discovered later) Quarrier's list of names showed that about a third of the group had accepted his offer. The Shoe-Black Brigade of Glasgow was in business. Headquarters were set up in Jamaica Street, in a room overlooking the Old Bridge. This was close enough to Quarrier's premises in Argyle Street to enable him to oversee things at the Brigade and carry on his own business as well. He engaged a man to teach the evening classes and personally saw to the kitting-out of each boy with a uniform, brushes, blacking and all the other tackle of the trade. Then Quarrier's boys took to the streets.

One of the early members of the Brigade was a wild lad named David Grey. He was fifteen when he volunteered for the Brigade, had no money in the world and had pawned most of his clothes. And yet, within a year, David was one of the top earners in the Brigade, sometimes bringing in thirty shillings a week and more, and had lost his reputation for gambling and roughness. He more than vindicated Quarrier's belief that support and organisation would bring out the best in even the most hardened street boy.

As the organisation grew, larger premises were needed. A move was first made to Bath Street and then to a large flat of six apartments at 114 Trongate, in the heart of the city. The membership of the Brigade had risen to a fairly steady 200 and the new premises had ample accommodation for schoolrooms and dormitories. The Brigade was doing well, earning its keep and gaining a reputation among its customers for tidiness, efficiency and good manners. Some years later Quarrier started a Newspaper Brigade, and then a Parcels Brigade, and for all the parcels and boxes entrusted to his boys at stations and offices there was never once a claim for damage or loss. In fact, the various Brigades were soon so successful that certain business interests in the city became rather alarmed. Some newspaper offices were not happy when Quarrier demanded reduced rates for his newspaper boys because, he said, he was a wholesaler, taking some 4,000 copies a day. And the licensed City Porters were none too thrilled at competition from the Parcels Brigade.

But, despite these frictions, Quarrier's Brigades continued to operate in the streets of Glasgow until the turn of the century, offering help, support and training to hundreds of young boys.

By 1870 William Quarrier had a string of shoe and boot shops in Glasgow and, between running his business and organising his Brigades,

Tontine Building, Trongate, 1868
(reproduced by courtesy of The Mitchell Library)

A Glasgow back-court (reproduced by courtesy of The Mitchell Library)

he was an extremely busy man. He had recently moved house to Kingston Place, on the south side of the city, and had a large household to support – his wife and four children, as well as the children of his younger sister, whose husband had died; when his sister died soon after her husband, Quarrier took care of the three children and brought them up as his own.

And yet Quarrier's work with the street boys of Glasgow had only convinced him that much more needed to be done. The city around him was a great metropolis of more than 450,000 souls, the second city of the Empire. Shipbuilding was growing and replacing the cotton trade as the city's main industry. The boundaries of the city were creeping farther and farther westwards and southwards and the slums of Quarrier's childhood were at last coming under the scrutiny of the public authorities with the establishment of the City Improvement Trust. The physical face of Glasgow had changed considerably since he was a young boy working in the Graeme Street pin factory; now, too, there was much more public concern about the plight of working children and of those orphaned and homeless. Conditions in the cotton mills and in the coalmines had been greatly improved by legislation regulating the number of working hours and the ages at which children could be employed. Since 1840 it had been illegal to employ anyone under twenty-one to go down the chimneys, and the days of sending young boys of seven or eight down narrow smoky flues were past. Homeless children under fifteen could now be taken off the streets by the courts and sent to Industrial Schools all over Scotland, where they would be fed and clothed and trained for a trade.

But though much had been achieved, the children of the streets remained. Quarrier saw them daily as he walked to work, when he visited his Brigade boys at their various posts around the city, and when he returned home at night. The same children Dickens has etched on our imaginations – Oliver Twist on the road to London, David Copperfield buying his ha'penny lunch of a stale pie after working for hours in the blacking factory, Jo the crossing sweeper in *Bleak House*, alone from morning to night, with no home and no family – these children were a fact of life on the streets of Glasgow. Some had lost one or both parents through the common diseases of tuberculosis, bronchitis and cholera; others were sent out to beg and steal for the family; others had simply left home and lived on the streets. The writer of the 1841 *Statistical Account* entry on Glasgow had noted that:

> . . . the number of orphans, and, what is worse, the number of children of depraved parents, thrown on the public without anyone to care for them, almost exceeds belief. *(p.217)*

By the last quarter of the century the situation was no better. Town authorities placed some children in the Poorhouse and boarded out many on farms or crofts in rural districts, but still the city's streets were full of homeless children. The reports of the Glasgow Society for the Prevention of Cruelty to Children, formed in 1884, recount case after case of children found wandering the streets, sleeping on stairheads and boxes and huddled against bakers' ovens. The following two cases are taken from a long list in the Society's 1886 Annual Report:

> *Case 114* M.G., a girl of twelve years of age, was found begging by the Superintendent and taken to the Shelter. On enquiries being made into her case it was found that both her parents were dead, and she was living by begging, without any proper home or guardian.

> *Case 203* D. McLean, twelve years of age. This boy was found selling papers and begging late at night by the officers of the Society. He stated that he had been supporting himself by begging, selling papers and carrying parcels at railway stations for a considerable time. His mother was dead and his father had deserted him. He had to sleep on stairs when he could not earn sufficient money to pay for his lodgings.

Quarrier wanted to help these children, not just by organising them into industrial brigades, but by giving them a home and the chance of a life away from the dangers and hardships of the streets. He had long had at the back of his mind a plan for a children's home in Glasgow. He knew of the work of George Müller, a Prussian pastor who had come to England in 1829 and opened an orphanage in Bristol six years later; he knew of Thomas Barnardo, who was working among the children of London's teeming streets. And he had met the formidable Annie Macpherson, a young woman from Glasgow who went to London in 1866 to help the poor people of the East End. In an empty warehouse in the city's Commercial Street she had set up a House of Industry, where hundreds of child matchbox-makers could work at their trade and receive food and education at the same time. Quarrier had met her when she visited Glasgow at the end of the 1860s, and was impressed with her account of the work in London; he was especially interested to hear of her Canadian emigration scheme for orphaned and destitute children, which she had started in 1869. She believed that such children would have a better chance in life if they were taken away from their miserable and impoverished surroundings and shipped out to work as farm hands and domestics in homesteads in Canada. Annie urged Quarrier to put his plans for a children's home into immediate action, and brushed aside his worries that he already had too much on his plate, with his family and his Brigades: God would support the work, she declared, and others would rally round.

Quarrier made up his mind to go ahead and on 31 August 1871 a second historic letter appeared in the *Glasgow Herald*. On 1 September the same letter, with minor variations, was published in the *North British Daily Mail*:

Sir,

For many years past I have been deeply impressed with the necessity that exists here for a Home for destitute boys, and I am persuaded that there is not one who moves about and notices the habits and surroundings of the boys of our streets but will be convinced that such a Home is needed. Many of your readers may not be aware of the vast number of houseless and homeless boys who receive shelter in our Night Asylum, and as this is one reason why we should have a Home, I beg to put before them the number who have received shelter during the past year which is, according to the report, 3,397. Giving three nights to each boy (which is the allotted time in the institution), this would give the number of 1,137 boys who either roam our streets or country without a home to cheer their desolate lives, or a house to cover their defenceless heads. Some have an easy way of getting out of their Christian responsibilities, and they say of these helpless ones, 'Send them to the Poorhouse'; others, to quiet their consciences, give a copper when they see the haggard face and tattered garments of the little urchin, and so the stream of neglected children goes on, deepening and deepening until God only knows what length it may reach. Fellow Christians and fellow citizens, should such things continue? I would say no, and thus I plead for a Home to which any boy may be sent, his case enquired into, and a helping hand extended to him until he is fit to labour for himself. It is only by such means that crime can be lessened in our juvenile population; for criminals are of the worst class who are so from their youth, and cost the country a thousand times more for the cure than for the prevention of crime. In fact, I believe it can't be cured, but I am sure that it might be prevented – not to speak of the disgrace to us that so many destitute children should be allowed to roam as they like amongst us, without let or hindrance. The amount of help rendered to the destitute boys of our streets by the Shoe-Black Society has been of great use to them and many hundreds have received help which has been a blessing to themselves and to the community, but one great want has been a Home to which orphan and destitute boys might be sent at once by any citizen who found them so, and to which an emigration scheme might be attached, so as to draft off to another land all who were fitted for it. Miss Macpherson, of London, has promised her practical cooperation and, with such help, there is no fear of success [sic]. Shall the practical help and sympathy of my fellow-citizens be wanting? I have no faith in large institutions where hundreds are ruled with a stringent uniformity which eats out the individuality of its members, but I have great faith in a Home where not more than one hundred are placed together, and where individual tastes would be cared for and watched over by a motherly and fatherly love. The Home I think we should begin with might cost from £1,000 to £2,000 to build and fit out, and if any of my fellow-citizens would feel inclined to put out this sum or any amount towards it, I feel certain that it would be laying up treasure in Heaven, where neither moth nor rust doth corrupt, and the blessing of those who are ready to perish would be sure to fall on their heads. The establishment of such a Home at the present time would be a fitting stone of remembrance of the Earl of Shaftesbury's visit to our city, and I have no doubt would meet with his hearty support and cooperation. Any communications or subscriptions towards the above object shall be duly acknowledged by

Yours truly,

W. Quarrier

It's a marvellous letter, at once passionate, practical and radical: by declaring, in an age of barrack-like workhouses, that he had no faith in large institutions but believed, instead, in preserving the individual, William Quarrier identified himself unmistakably as a man well ahead of his time.

Just twelve days later Quarrier received a letter promising the necessary money to buy or rent premises for the new Home. It came from a London businessman named Thomas Corbett. Corbett was already familiar with Quarrier's work with the Brigades, and Quarrier had indeed written to him personally about the need for an orphanage in Glasgow.

With the problem of money taken care of, Quarrier lost no time in looking for a suitable site for his Home and found it in Renfrew Lane, a little street running parallel to Sauchiehall Street. The place was small – just an old workshop – but Quarrier partitioned it off into a kitchen and sleeping area and tried to brighten up the bare brick walls with illuminated texts from the Bible. The Matron of the new Home was a Mrs Dunn. Like many other women who helped with sewing, mending, cooking and teaching, she had volunteered to work in the Home. Quarrier had met her some months before, in Porteous's Bookshop in Royal Exchange Square, where she worked and which he used to visit from time to time. One day he told her of his plans for a Home and asked if she would help out if his scheme materialised. She had promised her support, and for eight years she acted as Matron to hundreds of girls and boys.

Now the Renfrew Lane Home was ready to open and on 18 November 1871 the first boy stepped tentatively over the threshold. His name was Andrew, he had no jacket or shoes, and his first words as he padded across to the brightly burning fire in the corner were to enquire where everyone else was. He was followed the day after by Willie, a young boy, filthy and ragged, who had spent the last few nights in a cold tenement stairway. They were joined soon after by Jimmy, an orphan who had been deserted by his aunt and uncle and who scraped a living on the streets by selling matches and standing on his head for a ha'penny.

And so the list of names grew and the trickle of orphans and waifs became a stream. The children – boys and girls – ranged in age from four to fourteen; some were found by Quarrier and his helpers among the barrels and boxes at the harbour, in haylofts and stairways; some were brought, in varying degrees of wretchedness, filth and hunger, by missionary women and policemen; others turned up on the doorstep by themselves. Preference was given to orphans, then the children of widows, and lastly the children of what were called in those days 'dissolute parents' who were willing to hand them over into Quarrier's care. Every case was carefully enquired into – which sometimes ended up with a boy or girl being sent back to perfectly worthy parents from whom they had run away out of mischief.

A year after its opening the Renfrew Lane Home was so full that new premises had to be found. The boys were sent to Cessnock House, an old mansion house in spacious grounds in Govan Road, on the south side of the city, and the girls to new premises at 93 Renfield Street. Later this Home moved to another house, also in Govan Road. Corbett's original donation contributed towards the new houses and the rest was provided by money sent in by the public. One of Quarrier's worries about starting a Home of this kind had been money; he certainly could not afford to finance the work single-handed and each day children would have to be fed and clothed. But the money did come. Every day, gifts of a few pence, a shilling or several pounds poured in from all over the country: 'B.E., Glasgow, a sincere sympathiser, £10'; 'a Working Man, in stamps, 1s'; 'a Friend, Bridge of Allan, 5s' – in that first year alone, £1,399 15s 3d. As well as money, every day saw clothing, crockery, materials, food and furniture arriving from as far afield as London and Aberdeen. There is even a note in the 1872 Annual Report of a 'fine milk cow for Cessnock House', sent by Miss T. of Hillhead.

In the first year, ninety-three children entered the Home at Renfrew Lane. Thirty-five were sent to Canada as part of Annie Macpherson's emigration scheme (see chapter 5, 'The Golden Bridge'), one girl was adopted, two boys were drafted into the Shoe-Black Brigade, two returned to friends, one poor boy was sent to the Poorhouse because he was mentally unstable, and two boys ran away. At the end of the first year the Renfrew Lane Home was abandoned and every child was transferred either to Cessnock House or Renfield Street, which together had accommodation for about 100. The day-to-day routine at both places consisted of a mixture of formal lessons and chores or domestic tasks. With some fifty or sixty children in each Home, it was difficult to maintain much of the atmosphere of a family household which was Quarrier's ideal, but he saw to it that the children played together, helped around the house and worshipped together, morning and evening.

Most of the children in Cessnock House and Renfield Street did not stay for long but were almost immediately shipped off to Canada. But Quarrier also wanted to provide the means for rescuing children from the streets and training them for future lives and employment at home in Scotland. To do this, he had a plan for a new and special Home.

Chapter 3

Depriving the Poorhouse

... My early dreams and life's desire have been partly accomplished in the establishment of the Orphan Homes, but as there are a great many orphan children whom we have not been able to take up, and whom it is desirable to keep at home and train to useful occupations, I would like to see an Orphanage established near Glasgow on the cottage principle, to which children from any part of the country could be sent. By the cottage principle, I mean a number of cottages built near each other, say ten, each capable of accommodating twenty to thirty children, with a father and mother at the head of each household; playground and other appliances attached to each cottage, with a schoolhouse in the centre; also a central workshop; the father of each family to be able to teach a different trade, such as tailor, shoemaker, joiner, printer, baker, farmer, smith, etc; the mother to do the cooking for each household, with assistance if needed. Boys from the tailor's household wishing to learn shoemaking, could be sent to the shoemaker's workshop: or boys from the farmer's, wishing to learn joiner work, could be sent to the joiner's workshop; and so on, interchanging according to the trade best suited to the boy. The children would meet all together at school and church, and on special occasions in the common playground, but at other times in their own playground. It is desirable to keep up the family and home feeling amongst the children, and we believe this cannot be done in large institutions where hundreds of children are ruled by the stringent uniformity necessary where large numbers are gathered together for years.

This was William Quarrier's plan for a new Home, described in the first *Narrative of Facts* – an annual account of his work – in 1872. He was proposing nothing less than the construction of an entire village for children, complete with houses, shops and a school. It was a bold, ambitious scheme which must have caused even William Quarrier moments of doubt when he contemplated all the money and labour involved; he calculated that the purchase of the land and construction of the buildings would cost £20,000, a truly enormous sum in those days. Many skilled men and women would be needed and a vast amount of planning and work would be necessary in the selection of a suitable site.

And yet, for all its scale and magnitude, this latest plan was the natural progression and development of Quarrier's work. He had started with Industrial Brigades to organise and support the many young boys who scraped a meagre living on the streets. Then had come the Homes in Renfrew Lane and later Govan Road, which gave shelter to hundreds of homeless and orphaned children and tried to help them to a better life – by sending them to Canada or by placing them in situations at home, recruiting them for the Brigades or just providing a roof over their heads until something could be found. Now Quarrier wanted to give the children a more permanent home where they could live and grow, somewhere that looked and felt more like 'home' than a Home. Of course, by modern standards, twenty or thirty children in one cottage is far too many; but by comparison with the orphanages and poorhouses of his day, where hundreds ate together in huge halls and slept in large impersonal dormitories, the numbers Quarrier was proposing were innovatively small.

The idea of housing orphaned and needy children in cottages was not entirely new. There were no examples of it in Scotland, but Quarrier probably knew of the work of a Miss Meredith in England, who founded the Princess Mary's Village in Addlestone, Surrey, in 1871; there girls lived in groups of ten in cottages run by a house-mother and assisted by an older girl. The original idea for cottage homes had come from the continent; one example was the 'Rauhes Haus' of the German theologian Johann Wichern, opened near Hamburg in 1833. This was a group of cottages where young boys who had been in trouble or involved in crime lived together in small groups under adult supervision.

Quarrier was not alone in his conviction that large institutions were not the place to bring up children and that they needed to be in smaller groups in a homelier, more intimate atmosphere. Dr Barnardo was to come to the same conclusion just a few years later when he opened his first cottage home for girls at Barkingside, Essex, in 1876; his previous experience of running a large orphanage had shown him that sixty girls living under the same roof had no chance of improving and developing. He eventually decided that a more family-like set-up with smaller numbers was needed, and in his memoirs he described his new vision:

> There should be no longer a great house in which sixty of these motherless girls would be herded together, clad in some dull uniform generally divested of all prettiness; but little cottages should arise, each of them presided over by its own 'mother' and in which all the members of the family could be clad as working people's children were under ordinary circumstances. The girls should be of all ages, from the baby of a few months or weeks to the growing girls, some of whom would be nearly out of their teens. There family life and family love might be reproduced, and gentle, modest ways would be made possible in the retirement of the cottage with its four or five rooms, and under the influence of godly women who I was sure would come to my aid in due time.

Quarrier's original plan was for cottages to accommodate between twenty and thirty children of different ages. Each cottage would be headed by men and women with a committed Christian faith (this was the main stipulation) – a married couple for the boys' cottages and a single woman for the girls'. The children would all help around the house, cleaning, washing and making beds, the older ones helping with the cooking and looking after the young ones. Each cottage would function independently of the others, as a family household, but the children would mix at school and church. In these family groups, with firm discipline, congenial surroundings and a strong dose of Christian teaching, Quarrier believed that even the most wretched and the roughest of children could be trained and educated and given a chance for a better future.

Twenty thousand pounds was a huge sum of money to raise, and the initial response was very slow. By the following year only £88 had been sent in. But Quarrier was confident that the rest would come, just as everything necessary arrived daily for the feeding, clothing and educating of the 180 children admitted so far to the Glasgow Homes. In the meantime Quarrier had other schemes afoot.

" Inasmuch as ye have done it unto one of the least of these, ye have done it unto me."

A NARRATIVE OF FACTS

RELATIVE TO WORK DONE FOR CHRIST

IN CONNECTION WITH THE

ORPHAN AND DESTITUTE CHILDREN'S

EMIGRATION HOMES, GLASGOW,

FOR THE YEAR ENDING 31st OCTOBER, 1873.

BY

WILLIAM QUARRIER.

BOYS' HOME,
CESSNOCK HOUSE,
GOVAN ROAD.

———

CHILDREN'S NIGHT REFUGE
MISSION HALL
EAST GRÆME STREET.

GIRLS' HOME,
93 RENFIELD STREET.

———

IN CONNECTION WITH
MISS MACPHERSON'S
DISTRIBUTING HOMES,
CANADA.

" Naked, and ye clothed me."

GLASGOW:

GEORGE GALLIE & SON, 99 BUCHANAN STREET.

AIRD & COGHILL, 263 ARGYLE STREET.

PRICE THREEPENCE.

The cover page of Quarrier's second Annual Report

The first Saturday of 1873 had seen the opening of his Night Refuge for children and working lads. This was the first of its kind in Glasgow. There was already a City Night Asylum which took in some children, but it was mainly for men and women. Quarrier's Night Refuge was housed in the upper storey of an old church at the top of Dovehill, bordering Graeme Street, where he had worked as a boy. The floor was partitioned off into a large public area, a kitchen and a dormitory with twenty beds.

In the first ten months of its existence the Refuge gave shelter to 2,137 refugees – or rather, provided 2,137 'bed nights'; some children came for more than one night, and these Quarrier tried to help by sending them to his Brigades or to the Govan Road Homes. In the hall, which could accommodate 400 people, Quarrier held twice-weekly evangelistic meetings, which were open to the public. The hall was also used as a Reading Room for working men, and once a week there were 'sewing nights' for widows who needed to earn a little extra money. The sight of all the women must have stirred memories for Quarrier of the many nights, all those years ago in a High Street close, which his mother had spent painstakingly sewing tiny buttons and frills on to muslin and silk.

By 1874 Quarrier had several branches of work going on in the city: his Industrial Brigades were thriving, the Homes in Govan Road continued to send children to Canada, and the Dovehill Mission opened its doors every day to the hungry, the homeless, the poor and the widowed. By this time, too, there was enough money in the cottage homes kitty for Quarrier to start looking for a suitable site. He had £4,688 in hand with which to buy some land near Glasgow, in pleasant countryside, somewhere big enough for future expansion and with plenty of open space for the children. Part of Lord Blantyre's estate at Cardonald, on the southern boundary of the city (the site now occupied by Craigton cemetery), seemed to fit the bill. Quarrier began negotiations to buy the land in December 1874, but the bill of sale was never signed.

The *Narrative of Facts* for that year gives no explanation for the breakdown of the deal, but in his book, *A Romance of Faith* (1937), Alexander Gammie writes that it was on account of a wall which Lord Blantyre insisted should be built round the land he was selling.

Quarrier was agreeable to this but only on condition that the wall was not entirely on *his* side, and that Lord Blantyre build part of it on his. Lord Blantyre flatly refused, so Quarrier decided to look elsewhere.

The breakdown in negotiations occurred in May 1875 and it was not until nearly a year later that another site was chosen. At the beginning of April 1876 an advertisement appeared in the newspapers announcing the sale of Nittingshill Farm near the little Renfrewshire village of Bridge of Weir, to the west of Paisley. The sale was to be held on 26 April; so on a cold, rainy day earlier that month, Quarrier travelled out to Bridge of Weir to have a look at the land. The village was about sixteen miles from the centre of Glasgow, and the farm of Nittingshill lay two miles beyond that. Even in the pouring rain it was a beautiful spot: forty acres of rich green fields and woodland, with the rolling Kilbarchan hills to the south and the rivers Cattie and Gryffe forming a natural boundary to the estate. Here the children would be deep in the Renfrewshire countryside, and yet there was easy connection with Glasgow by rail.

It was everything Quarrier had been looking for; as he stood surveying the land, in his mind's eye he could see his little village taking shape. There would be an administrative block in the centre, with a communal hall, schoolrooms and workshops. He would range the ten cottages in a rough circle round the central building, each with its own garden and connected by wide avenues. And then there would be space for cultivating crops to feed the big family and, of course, a playing area. Yes, it was the perfect spot.

The date of the sale found Quarrier excited and hopeful that there would be no competition from other buyers. However, there was another interested buyer who bid against him consistently and Quarrier soon found that he was not to get his land without a bit of a tussle. Slowly the price increased by £5 and £10, see-sawing from one man to the other, until Quarrier eventually won and bought the 40 acres for £3,560 – £560 more than the reserve price. He immediately vested the land with a group of trustees, among them Thomas Corbett, the man who had donated the original £2,000 for Renfrew Lane.

This same group of men also acted as trustees for another piece of land Quarrier had acquired earlier in the year when he had opened his City Home in James Morrison Street, a purpose-built five-storey

The City Home, James Morrison Street

apartment block which housed the entire Dovehill organisation. The premises at Dovehill had been bought by the School Board; but thanks to the generosity of two Glasgow ladies, who met the entire cost of £10,000, new ground at James Morrison Street was bought and built upon. These remarkably generous women are not named in the *Narrative of Facts*, but Alexander Gammie in *A Romance of Faith* identifies them as a Mrs Robert Smith and her daughter, Mrs Alexander Allan.

All in all, 1876 was a good year for William Quarrier. He had his new City Home, with accommodation for a hundred working lads and temporary shelter for forty destitute women, a shelter for homeless children and a mission hall. Most importantly, he had at last purchased the ground for Scotland's first cottage homes for children.

The next thing was to start building. Quarrier and his architect, Robert Bryden, envisaged the Central Building in a functional Gothic style with turreted roof, pointed gables and plain uncarved walls. The building would be three-storeyed with schoolrooms, workrooms and storerooms on the ground floor. The first floor would have a large

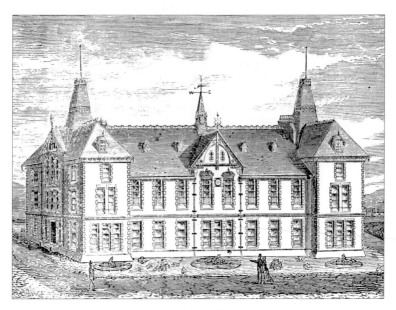

Central Building

hall for services and rooms for the teachers. Until there were enough cottages Quarrier also intended using the top floor for sleeping quarters for the children.

The plan was for the Homes to be formally opened once the Central Building and two cottages, one on either side, had been completed. Each cottage would be built in a style harmonising with the Central Building, but Quarrier also specified that the cottages were all to be slightly different from one another so as to be more like individual houses with their own characters. He also wanted them to reflect the national character of the Homes. They were to be for children from every part of Scotland, so he suggested in the 1876 *Narrative of Facts* that different towns and cities across the country should donate the money to build a cottage which would be named after them. Individuals might want to build a cottage in memory of a relative, and

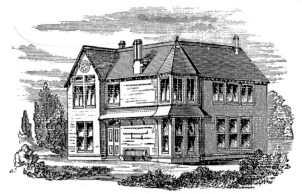

ORPHAN COTTAGE HOMES OF SCOTLAND.

TO HOUSE 300 ORPHAN AND DESTITUTE CHILDREN, TO COST £20,000.

CHILDREN'S COTTAGE.

The above is a sketch of one of the proposed Cottages prepared by a friend. The house is about 39 feet square. The ground floor consists of parlour, 15 by 12 feet, for father, mother, and visitors; children's nursery or play-room, 18 by 14 feet; dining-room, 18 by 14 feet; kitchen, 14 by 12 feet; scullery, pantry, bath-room, &c. Top flat consists of bed-room for father and mother, 15 by 12 feet; No. 1 dormitory, 18 by 14 feet; No. 2 dormitory, 18 by 14 feet; No. 3 dormitory, 14 by 12 feet; spare bed-room, 7½ by 6 feet; wall wardrobes for children's clothing, &c. Each cottage is to accommodate not more than thirty children, and the expected cost is about £1000.

Reproduced from the 1875 Narrative of Facts

organisations such as the Sabbath Schools of Scotland could use their collection money specially for a cottage at Bridge of Weir.

Although Quarrier made the financial needs of his organisation known to the readers of his *Narrative of Facts*, he would not advertise publicly for funds, unlike, for example, Dr Barnardo in London, who was a great showman and publiciser of his work. Quarrier would approve no fund-raising bazaars or musical entertainments or any other advertising efforts, and he would not employ collectors. He believed that the work in which he was engaged was God's work and that a simple statement of needs in the *Narrative of Facts* and constant prayer would secure whatever was necessary.

But William Quarrier was not a man to pray and leave it at that. He was a successful businessman, a man of tremendous energy, enthusiasm and determination who worked tirelessly towards his goals. There is a story about him in Gammie's *A Romance of Faith* which perfectly illustrates Quarrier's balance between faith and self-help:

> One Monday morning Mr Quarrier was driving the weekend preacher to Bridge of Weir station. As they entered the village, the train was seen approaching, and it seemed doubtful if they would be in time. The preacher, in his anxiety lest he should lose the train, excitedly exclaimed: 'Don't you think we should pray about it, Mr Quarrier?' 'No, not yet,' replied Mr Quarrier, as he cracked the reins, 'wait till we see what the horse can do.' (*p.144*)

For me, that's the real man. I can almost hear the grim amusement in his tone as he restrains his friend's anxious fervour.

Quarrier's architect, Robert Bryden, worked hard at the plans for the new cottage homes and building began in February 1877 with the laying of the foundation stone of the first cottage. It was to be called 'Broadfield' and the £1,300 for its construction had been promised in a letter Quarrier had received just six months after the purchase of Nittingshill. The money was gifted by a couple from Port Glasgow in memory of their son; in June of the following year another £1,300 was donated by a lady from Glasgow, in memory of her mother, for a second cottage, to be called 'Glasgow Home'.

Building went on throughout 1877, and by early 1878 work on the Central Building was well under way. The total cost was to be £4,800;

but the building fund was short by some £1,300 and when the balance was still outstanding by springtime, Robert Bryden became rather anxious. He suggested to Quarrier that work should be suspended until the rest of the money materialised, but the answer was no: Quarrier believed the money would come in time.

This was a trying time for Quarrier; he was not made any easier in his mind by the prospect of having to leave the scene at this critical stage, for he was due to accompany that year's party of children to Canada – the seventh group of children to make the journey since the Renfrew Lane Home opened. The departure date was 2 May, and by late April the outstanding £1,300 still had not appeared. Quarrier had never been away from his work for more than a week; now he was going to be on the other side of the Atlantic for two or three months. It was not that people like Robert Hunter, the Superintendent of Cessnock Home, or the Matron of Renfield Home or the many volunteers who helped in the work were not competent; but it was hard for Quarrier to leave others in charge of all the projects which he had conceived, planned, organised and directed from the beginning. But his wife was particularly anxious for him to have a break from the constant strain of running everything and, besides, some changes were being made in the Canadian end of the emigration scheme which made it necessary for him to go out and oversee things.

Two days before the SS *Phoenician* was due to steam out from Mavisbank Quay (on the south bank of the river), Quarrier received a visit from a friend named Alexander Thomson, a retired farmer and bachelor, who had taken a keen interest in the Homes work from the outset. 'I had been intending to give £1,300 for the erection of a cottage' he said, 'but I'd like to donate it towards the Central Building instead'. So the Central Building account was finally balanced and Quarrier could look forward to the official opening of his new Orphan Homes soon after he returned from Canada in July.

The date announced in the newspapers for the official opening of 'Mr Quarrier's Orphan Homes of Scotland at Bridge of Weir' was 17 September 1878. The wet, stormy weather which caused some damage to the roof of the newly completed Central Building did not deter the hundreds of people who flocked there on the great day. They crammed the special train from Glasgow and arrived in droves from Greenock, Port Glasgow and all over the country. Well before the official proceedings began at two o'clock the hall was jammed tight with people; many stood in the aisles and others, crowded together at the back, had to crane their necks for a view of the platform party.

Quarrier made a sparkling address to the hundreds gathered there that day, among them Dr Barnardo and Provost Lyle of Greenock. He stood before them, correct and sombre in his dark frock coat, his shrewd, rather stern gaze warm with enthusiasm, and declared, 'I am here to testify that God has not failed me at any time'. He talked of hope and faith in the future and of the gifts from people all over the country which had made the day possible, from 'the widow's mite to the merchant prince's thousand'. He told his listeners that in the last seven years, 700 children had been rescued from the streets of Glasgow and £34,000 had been donated to feed, clothe, educate and look after them. And, in an aside specially designed to encourage businessmen, he revealed that only 5 per cent of that money had been spent on helpers and workers.

Everyone who heard him must have been stirred by his energy and vision. His plan was for ten cottages to be built in the next few years, but his strong hope was that during his lifetime or after, many more would be added. Looking round the hall he declared, 'My earnest desire is to deprive the poorhouse of as many children as possible'; and with thunderous applause ringing in his ears, William Quarrier looked boldly to the future.

Mr and Mrs Quarrier

Chapter 4

A Children's City

Just four years after the grand opening of the Orphan Homes of Scotland, William Quarrier had achieved his goal of ten cottages. The original nucleus of buildings – the Central Building, Broadfield Home, Glasgow Home and an unfinished third cottage, Dalry Home – had been joined by seven more cottages: the Dunbartonshire, Ebenezer, Washington, Aberdeen, Greenock, Anderston and Paisley Homes, each the gift of an individual and together housing 300 children, from toddlers to twelve-year-olds.

And Quarrier had surpassed his original dream, by giving the village an invalids' home and a complex of buildings housing workshops and washing facilities. He had also received promises of more gifts to build more cottages.

In fact the Orphan Homes of Scotland were so successful, and growing at such a rate, that Quarrier had to give up his shoemaking business in Glasgow and devote himself entirely to the work. He was the motivating force, the inspiration and the sole manager of a vast organisation which now stretched from the smoky centre of Glasgow to the green hills of Renfrewshire and across the Atlantic to Canada. The increasing workload had forced him to give up one of his three shops as early as 1875, and four years later he relinquished another part of his business. Finally, in 1882, he decided that the last of his shops would have to go; eighteen hours a day spent managing the Orphan Homes simply left no time to run a business.

But where was his own income to come from? His friends pointed out that he had always been sublimely confident that all the necessary money for the Homes would come from God when needed – so why not rely on the same source to provide for the needs of himself and his family and trust that money would be sent in specifically for that purpose? Quarrier announced his decision in the *Narrative of Facts* in 1882:

> I believe God will supply, so have decided to depend on Him in the time to come for all that I require for myself and family. This explanation is necessary, as some are under the impression that I have money invested and that I live partly off the Homes. Such is not the case. I have no invested capital, nor have I ever, at any time, lived off the Homes. The opposite is the fact, as a considerable portion of my own means have been given and spent in the interests of the work. For the future I have resolved to continue in the same course, i.e. not to touch anything belonging to the Homes but to depend entirely on the Lord to send what I require for myself and family. I do not say everyone should do as I have done, but if they are led by the Lord in the same way as I have been there is no other course left open to them.

Four years later money was sent in to build a house on the premises at Bridge of Weir for Quarrier and his family to live in. They called it 'Homelea' and the building is still there today, just inside the main drive, converted to offices which are let to a local accountancy firm.

The Orphan Homes of Scotland continued to grow. In 1884 three new cottages – Cessnock, Mizpah and Leven – were completed to house the children from the Govan Road Homes which were now proving too small and were discontinued. At the dedication service for these latest cottages Quarrier declared:

> We have only touched the borders of the orphans of the land. They are there by the thousand. I intend, God willing, to double the number of cottages – that is to say, instead of seventeen houses, to have thirty-four. In other words, instead of spending as we have been doing £40,000 in these buildings, we intend to spend £80,000.

He was as good as his word and as cottage followed cottage, and acre after acre of land was drained, levelled and built upon, by the early years of the 1890s the target of thirty-four cottages was in sight. What had once been forty green acres of Nittingshill farm was now a

A sketch from the 1896 Narrative of Facts

thriving community of forty-six buildings and more than 800 children – a 'children's city' as the *North British Daily Mail* called it in an article of 1890. Anyone could come and visit, every day of the week except Sunday. A train from St Enoch's in Glasgow would whisk the visitor to Bridge of Weir; from there it was a short carriage ride to the Orphan Homes where the Superintendent, Mr McFadzean, would give a guided tour.

At the main entrance to the Homes were two great gates (long gone today) which opened inwards onto a broad avenue lined with young trees and shrubs and stretching away to the Central Building in the distance. This was Faith Avenue. To the right and left, along its length, stood cottage after cottage, each with its own front lawn and flower patch – Oswald Invalid Home for Girls, Paisley Home, Aberdeen Home, Washington Home. Over to the right down by the Cattie Burn was the laundry and next door the workshops, always a hive of activity, where joiners, printers, shoemakers and bakers, most of them cottage fathers, worked all day.

Further on, a gently sloping road led up Faith Avenue to Mount Zion – a huge church in Victorian style, with a 120-foot tower. The

OPENING OF NEW CHURCH AT BRIDGE-OF-WEIR HOMES.
(Reprinted from "North British Daily Mail," 7th March, 1888.)

A large and handsome church, which has been planted amid the Orphan Homes of Scotland at Bridge-of-Weir, was opened yesterday. The event was rightly regarded by Mr. Quarrier, the founder of that most interesting of all colonies, as one of great importance in the history of the beneficent work to which he has devoted all his means, his time, his great organising power, and his marvellous faith. The visible results of that work must appear almost incredible to those who only hear about and don't see them. Since it began 17 years ago, 5,000 children have passed through these Homes and the Homes in Glasgow, and of these 2,500 have been sent to Canada with a full stock of health, a capital training, and plenty of good clothes. On the property, beautifully situated among the Renfrewshire hills, some two miles from Bridge-of-Weir, where the country Homes are, there was only a farmhouse twelve years ago. Now, however, the old farmhouse has disappeared, and there are on the ground

No fewer than 28 Buildings

Reproduced from the 1888 Narrative of Facts

church was built in 1888 with £5,000 from an anonymous donor. With a seating capacity of 1,000 it could cope with the growing family of children and provided grander surroundings for the services, which had previously been held in the Central Building. All around Mount Zion were more cottages facing on to Hope Avenue and behind it, Love Avenue – Montrose Home, Allan Dick Home, Edinburgh Home and many others.

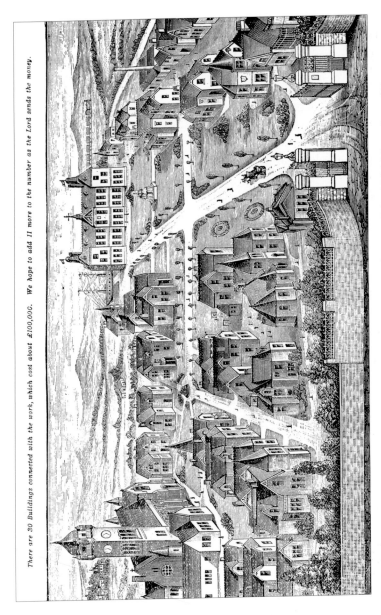

There are 30 Buildings connected with the work, which cost about £100,000. We hope to add 11 more to the number as the Lord sends the money.

Reproduction of a woodcut illustration from the inside back cover of the 1888 Narrative of Facts

Every cottage and each gift of money had a story behind it. The Sabbath School Home was built with the thousands and thousands of pennies collected by Sabbath Schools all over Scotland. Jehovah-Jireh Home was the result of an anonymous donation of £2,000 in banknotes which was left one morning on Quarrier's desk. Another morning he found among his mail a large bulky envelope containing dozens and dozens of banknotes totalling £1,700 and a note which said simply, 'From Sagittarius'. The donor requested that the money be used to build and furnish a cottage to be designated 'The Gift of Sagittarius, Greenock'.

Quarrier would generally accept any name for the cottage suggested by the donor, but there was one occasion where he did not approve of the choice of name. The donor of the fourth cottage, Dunbartonshire, originally wanted it to be called 'Quarrier Home' – but Quarrier would have none of it. As far as he was concerned the Homes were God's, not his. I wonder what he would feel today if he knew that the entire organisation had been named after him.

One of the most remarkable donations made to the Homes was from Jane Stewart, an old woman who lived in Main Street, Gorbals. On 26 March 1891 a friend of Quarrier's asked him if he would come and meet an old lady who wanted to make a contribution towards the work. Quarrier duly went to call upon Jane Stewart in her tidy little Gorbals single-end, where she told him the story of her difficult, lonely life as a servant and washerwoman. She ended by saying that she wished to give something to help the Homes work. Looking round her spartan room Quarrier naturally expected very little, but to his astonishment she rummaged about in a chest of drawers and produced a wad of bank receipts, totalling more than £600! Fearing that he might be depriving the old woman of her entire life's savings, Quarrier gently asked if the gift were not too much. 'Na, na, I've plenty mair, an ye'll get it a' when I dee' she replied, and pushed the bundle into his hands.

Just two days later Jane Stewart died. She left more than £1,000 to the Orphan Homes of Scotland, made up of a deposit receipt for £400, savings in the bank of £200, £27 15s in cash and fifty-five shares in the Lancashire Insurance Company bought twenty years before and now worth more than £400. All this was the thrifty accumulation of

The 'James Arthur' training ship

fifty-five years of meagre earnings as a servant and washerwoman. As a fitting tribute to this remarkable old woman, her money was used towards the provision of a new piped water-supply for the Homes.

The gifts which arrived on Quarrier's desk every day were not just for the building of cottages. The Orphan Homes were much more than a collection of houses. Behind the Central Building a training ship was erected, the *James Arthur*, a fully-rigged vessel cemented to the ground in which some thirty boys lived and worked as part of their training for a career in the merchant navy. The Homes had their own school and their own poultry farm. There was a park down by the River Gryffe with swings and seesaws, and an outdoor swimming pond in the Cattie. And down by the workshops were greenhouses to grow all kinds of vegetables for the large family, as well as stables and a coach house.

Quarrier had the mammoth task of maintaining this extraordinary village and providing for the hundreds of men, women and children who lived and worked in it. And yet he never knew, from one day to the next, if he would have sufficient funds. Daily maintenance of the City Home and the Orphan Homes was about £40 in the early 1890s; but Quarrier was very strict about using the gifts which were sent to him each day. His rule was that money could only be used for the purpose specified by the donor, so that if £10 were sent in for the Bridge of Weir Building Fund when he needed £10 for food, he could only use it towards building costs. Furthermore, there was never any money comfortably gathering interest in the bank, which could be drawn on in emergencies, because Quarrier would not allow the stockpiling of funds. Every penny sent was ploughed into the work, so that anyone who donated money would know that it was being used directly and effectively. For this reason Quarrier would not accept any endowments for the future maintenance of the Homes, and in 1881 he had to refuse £8,000 offered in this way for one of the cottages. He trusted completely in unsolicited gifts from generous people and his trust was not let down – the children never went hungry or cold; but often the financial year closed only just on the right side – in 1888 a balance of 11s 4½d! And many a day his diary made anxious reading:

Aug. 2 Only 12 shillings today, and our wants are many.

Aug. 4 From Dumbarton £100. This was needed and has greatly cheered us.

As the cottages were built, the children filled them, arriving daily from the City Home in James Morrison Street, which acted as a receiving centre. Every child's case was looked into there, and the particulars taken down, before admission to Bridge of Weir. The qualifications for entry to the Orphan Homes were listed on the back of every *Narrative of Facts*:

Bridge of Weir, Renfrewshire – Orphan boys and girls deprived of both parents, children of widows, or others with no relative able or willing to keep them, from one to fourteen years of age, from any part of the country. Destitution is the title for admission, and there is no subscriber's line or voting paper required.

An up-to-date file was kept on every single child who was registered at the City Home, and the notes fill volume after volume. It's not known if Quarrier himself wrote the early files, but it would certainly be in keeping with his energy and the personal interest he took in every aspect of the work. But whoever wrote them, these Diaries of Admission are not just a catalogue of misery and poverty, or neglected children in their thousands; each page is a portrait of a real person. Reading the faded entries, beautifully hand-written on the thick,

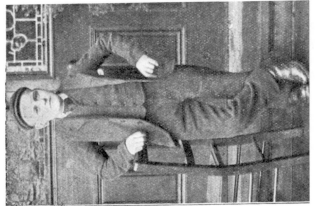

H.T., a Physical Miracle, without the Surgeon's Aid, as sent to Canada, 1897

The Narrative of Facts frequently carried this kind of Before and After illustration of the children who came to Bridge of Weir

H.T., a Physical Wreck through want and neglect, as received, 1886

musty-smelling pages of enormous bound notebooks, is like looking at very old black-and-white photographic portraits: the sense of the past is strong and yet there is also a thrilling depth and immediacy. Here are a few of the entries from the volume of 1890 to 1891:

HUNTER, ROBERT

1890

Dec 5 Robert says he is fourteen past.

He is sent here by Charity Organisation Society to whom he was sent by a Dr at Western Infirmary Dispensary where he went on account of broken out head. Dr says it is caused by neglect and quite curable. His story is that he walked from Linlithgow where he lived for some time but has been wandering all about since his father left eighteen months ago. He heard father Wm, a brassfinisher, has gone to America. Mother dead four years. He is taken meantime and COS will make enquiry. He can't read.

1891

Jan 28 Dismissed on this date and fare paid to Linlithgow where he says he can find some friends. Letter of enquiry sent by COS was returned so that he is evidently not truthful. A collection box in hall was broken open a few nights ago while he was door-boy (there was no money in it) and he had been spending money of which he could not give very satisfactory account. His honesty was doubted and as nothing could be found out about his friends the above course was thought best.

In the house he was quiet, obliging and well-behaved.

STEVENSON, DUNCAN

1890

Nov 27 Duncan born 7 July 1881 at 41 Hospital St Gorbals. He seems a poor 'subject'. He wants an eye, has a lisp and is only on sixth book. He had measles and whooping cough. Father Robert Gillespie Stevenson a carter, 25 N Coburg St, is unable to work with chronic Bronchitis and his wife Eliz. M.S. Murray is a cripple from paralysis so that they propose going into Poor House to see whether or not they regain strength sufficient to do some work. Father signs emigration form (X).

Letter of recommendation from Wm Gilford, 114 Hospital St, who has known them for four years.

Given back to father who for some reason known to himself regretted leaving him here.

WALLACE, GEORGE

1890

Dec 13 George is said to be sixteen years of age.

He had hip-joint disease and in consequence uses a crutch. He does not look strong. On account of his health and also as parents could afford to give him a light job he has not been at work but having musical talent he was being taught violin-playing with view of making it a profession.

As circumstances have changed he wishes to earn a living by tailoring or brush-making and although rather old not to have been at work he seems a decent lad and promises to do as wanted.

Parents dead. Mother died in June and since then a brother Wm, a druggist

living at 94 Main St Rutherglen, has kept him but can't continue as he has broken down in health, and is being treated for chest disease in Western Infirmary – Koch treatment – and has been idle five months. Wm is married. He brings Geo. here.
1896
Aug. 21 To lodgings. His apprenticeship as a tailor with David Angus, York St, is finished. He is still very delicate.
1897
Jan. Married to Effie Kin (?).
1907
Feb. 17 George died this date of consumption.

What happened to all those thousands of children whose lives appear briefly on the pages of the Diaries of Admissions? The matter-of-fact notes are vivid and poignant precisely because they are so dry and brief; it doesn't take much imagination to read all the human sorrow and hope and suffering between the lines.

After registration at the City Home it was decided where the child should be sent – either to one of the Brigades, or perhaps to the Working Lads' Home or to Bridge of Weir. At Bridge of Weir a child would be placed in a cottage with thirty or more other boys or girls. The daily routine was necessarily strictly governed, with rising-time, meals, chores and family worship an unchanging part of the controlled timetable. But Quarrier always aimed to have individuality and family feeling as much as possible among the children; there were no uniforms or any kind of strange garb which would brand the children as orphans and Homes boys and girls. The ages in each cottage ranged from toddlers upwards, and Quarrier hoped that this, too, would foster a sense of friendship and family.

Each cottage marched to school in the morning in an orderly group. Elementary education was given, as well as sewing classes for the girls. By the 1890s the Education (Scotland) Act of 1872 was well in force and school attendance between the ages of five and thirteen was compulsory, although it would still be many years before all parents did send their children to school. Once his children were past school age, Quarrier saw to it that they received some sort of training for a trade. The boys could be apprenticed to the joiners, printers, carpenters and shoemakers who worked in the village and the girls trained for domestic

Classes in the old schoolroom of the Central Building
(reproduced from Urquhart's Life Story of William Quarrier)

Registered for Transmission Abroad.

The Bailie.

"MY CONSCIENCE!"

No. 414. Glasgow, Wednesday, September 22nd, 1880. Price 1d

MEN YOU KNOW—No. 414.

TO seek the good of our fellow-men is, as we all know, the most elevated of human pursuits. The profession of a philanthropist enables you, to use a phrase which used to be commoner a couple of decades ago than it is to-day, to make the best of both worlds. You not only get unlimited credit in this life by your deeds, but their savour lasts even unto the life which is to come. Philanthropists, to be sure, are seldom to be reckoned among the most likeable of mortals. If his biographers may be believed, John Howard was a harsh father and an indifferent friend. History, indeed, is generally silent as to the individual excellencies of people of the Howard class. Before you can set up as a philanthropist, you must not only be possessed by a notion that the people round about you are a poor lot, but that you yourself are a person of pre-eminent virtue. It would be impossible to preserve the position of a philanthropist were you to come down from your pedestal, even for a day, and believe that you were no more than as are those whom you have set yourself to succour and save. It is one thing, however, to watch the weaknesses of philanthropists—their inordinate vanity, their dislike of opposition, the bitterness they display toward all who take up a like *rôle* with themselves—and another to contemn the work they have set themselves to do. Our friend WILLIAM QUARRIER, for instance, is one of the purest-minded and most earnest men living. His whole life is devoted to a noble end, and it may be questioned whether any other single individual has really effected more good in this city of ours during the last ten years than that which has resulted from his individual efforts. Personally, however, Mr QUARRIER is susceptible of a large degree of improvement.

VOL. XVI.

He is imperious beyond everything. No rival is allowed to approach within bowing distance even of his throne. He simply will not tolerate criticism. Whatever savours of mirth or gaiety finds in him a sworn foe. To people, besides, whose ideas are of the humbler sort, he seems to live and move in an atmosphere of absolute and even outrageous irreverence. He has so accustomed himself to regard Providence as a species of adjunct to his schemes for ameliorating the condition of our city Arabs, that his addresses to the Higher Powers are couched in the form of command rather than of supplication. The BAILIE respects Mr QUARRIER with an exceeding great respect; but if some measure of sweetness—it were too much to ask for light—were mingled with the unwearied devotion, the unselfish effort which marks his every-day work, how worthy he would be of liking as well as admiration. He counts it gain to spend and be spent in the cause of the needy and the suffering; but the narrowness of his view, the intensity of his egotism, give serious cause for annoyance to the more earnest among us and supply those of an irreverent temper with material for amusement, and occasionally for even scoffing and laughter. Mr QUARRIER'S first public efforts were made in connection with the shoe black brigade, the members of which were boarded, educated, and cared for under his supervision. The main work of his life, however, has been the erection of the Orphan Cottage Homes of Scotland at Bridge of Weir. These were started some eight years ago, and to-day forty acres of ground, and handsome cottages and villas capable of accommodating from two hundred to three hundred children, show a splendid result of Mr QUARRIER'S labours. Besides the Bridge of Weir Institution, Mr QUARRIER has started and superintend a boys' and girls' home at Cessnock House, near Govan; and

---

An extract from The Bailie, *a publication which was well known for its sharp comments on leading personalities of the day*
(reproduced by courtesy of The Mitchell Library)

service in the laundry and sewing rooms, as well as by helping with the running of the cottage. This was central to Quarrier's conviction that what these children needed was not just to be brought up in home-like surroundings, but also to be trained to find their own way honestly and successfully in life afterwards, and not be thrown back on the mercy of street and parish.

By 1897 there were thirty-seven cottages housing more than 900 children in the Orphan Homes. Since 1878, fifty-two buildings had been constructed and thousands of children had been helped. And still the money arrived each day, and still the work expanded. But it was not always plain sailing at Bridge of Weir, and Quarrier, who was an uncompromising man, incurred criticism from various quarters about the way he ran things. On one occasion the Catholic community of Glasgow accused him of proselytism and of withholding children whose parents or relatives were now in a position to look after them and wanted them back. He went to court over the matter and was completely exonerated; but there were others to question his firm and sometimes overbearing methods. The *Glasgow Herald,* always quick to criticise his work, claimed that he had too much power over an organisation which received its funds entirely from the public, and declared that the Homes should be run by a committee.

One of the biggest wrangles Quarrier was involved in was over the paying of rates to Renfrewshire County Council. The dispute began in 1896 and dragged on for more than six years. These were difficult times for Quarrier and the work of the Homes. When the row broke out other matters were also causing concern: an outbreak of scarlatina (a mild form of scarlet fever) among the children, and the failure of Quarrier's own health later that year due to the kidney trouble which was to dog him for years. In addition, the Homes had been taken to court by the proprietor of a neighbouring farm because of a drainage problem for which he blamed Quarrier. And the following year, 1897, emigration to Canada was stopped because of legislation passed in Ontario to which Quarrier took exception.

So amid all this, an argument with Renfrewshire County Council was the last thing Quarrier needed. For the past sixteen years the Orphan Homes had not paid any rates since they came under the 1869 'Sunday and Ragged School Act' which exempted from such taxation 'institutions for the gratuitous education of children and young persons of the poorest classes, without any pecuniary benefit being derived therefrom by the teacher'. The nineteenth century had seen many such Ragged Schools spring up all over Britain, following the example of John Pounds, a Portsmouth cobbler, who in 1818 held classes in the three Rs for the waifs and orphans around the docks there. D. Guthrie of Edinburgh published his *Plea for Ragged Schools* in 1847 and set up the city's first premises where the children of poor people could go to learn reading and writing and the basic skills of some trade, like shoemaking, as well as receiving free meals.

On a larger scale, this was what Quarrier was offering in the Orphan Homes and he considered the Homes very much a Ragged School. But suddenly, out of the blue, in 1896 the County Council of Renfrewshire announced its intention to claim back-rates and to start taxing the Homes in the normal fashion. Quarrier was very angry and refused to pay. The whole system at Bridge of Weir, he said, was and always had been based on the Ragged School – the teachers at the school received no guaranteed salary, all the workers were volunteers, and the sole source of funds was donations. The Homes themselves made no demands on the local council since they had their own water supply, their own bakery and handymen, and no claim was made on the Kilmacolm School Board for assistance in educating the children.

The matter went to the Court of Session, but the decision went against Quarrier. The judge pronounced, finely, that the Orphan Homes of Scotland were a 'large and very highly developed Ragged School', therefore more than a Ragged School, therefore liable for normal rating. The *Narrative of Facts* of 1898 seethes with Quarrier's indignation at the decision:

> The Ragged and Sunday Schools Act gives provision for holding meetings or classes, and doing other work of a voluntary kind; and this is what we contend for, that the whole concern is for the gratuitous education and feeding of the hungry, which this Act does not prohibit being done. Who can conceive of a child being educated who has no home to live in, and no moral surroundings: the thing is out of reason. Every Ragged School, from the first one of John Pounds the cobbler, down to the present day, has not withheld food as well as lodging for the homeless: and because we do our work better are we not to have the benefit of all that the law can do for us?

Quarrier appealed, but to no avail, and the following year he was ordered to pay five years of back-rates amounting to £800, £300 for the legal expenses of the Council, and his own expenses of £600.

This was galling enough; but then the Parish Council of Kilmacolm saw their chance and stepped in with a demand for four years of parish and school back-rates! And yet the School Board of Kilmacolm had never made any provision for the education of the Orphan Homes' children, let alone given assistance over the past four years. Furthermore, the Board would not assure Quarrier that if he paid the rates they would undertake the future education of his children. At a loss to understand their attitude, and incensed at the way in which he and his children were being treated, Quarrier declared war on the Kilmacolm Board. His strategy was typically bold and direct. One morning in April he marched the two miles along the road from the Homes to Kilmacolm at the head of a vast army of 800 of his children, column upon column of them, carrying banners and flanked by their cottage parents. Quarrier led his troops straight to Kilmacolm School where an irate member of the Board refused him admission. Undeterred, Quarrier turned to address the children and the interested crowd which had gathered. In a loud voice he explained the purpose of the protest – to draw attention to the Board's unfair and disgraceful actions – and finished with a formal demand that the School Board fulfil its responsibilities and educate his children. Then William Quarrier turned on his heel and marched back home, closely followed by his 800 children. It was a dramatic gesture which must have caused the Board acute embarrassment, but even so it was several years before the dispute was finally resolved.

Just before his death, in 1903, Quarrier arranged a meeting with the Board and, as a result of this, they took over responsibility for the education of the Homes children soon afterwards. It took a long time, but in the end Quarrier did win his battle for his children.

Chapter 5

The Golden Bridge

A rescue home must be continuously gathering in fresh inmates, else in a single generation it would be compelled to close its doors and write in the face of new applicants 'No admission'. But to secure the open door in front, it must maintain its exit door in the rear.[*]

So said Dr Thomas Barnardo to his trustees one day in the late 1870s as he outlined his plans for the emigration of English children to Canada. Canada, the New World, the infant country with great open spaces and untapped natural resources, was to be the 'exit door' for the thousands of pauper and orphaned children Barnardo had been rescuing from London's teeming streets. His boast was that no destitute child would ever be refused admission to his boys' home in Stepney or his girls' cottages in Barkingside; but this inevitably meant a constant stream of children to his door, and to cope with the increasing numbers Barnardo now began to look across the Atlantic to the farms and homesteads of Ontario, Quebec and Manitoba, where thousands of British children had already been settled by various charitable organisations. Those who sent the children spoke of a new life for them, a chance for a new future far away from the grime, overcrowding and poverty of Britain's industrial cities. They saw emigration as advantageous to the child,

---

[*] This statement by Dr Barnardo is taken from Kenneth Bagnell's book, *The Little Immigrants* (Macmillan of Canada, 1980, p.140), which has also provided much of the background for this chapter.

good for Canada – an expanding country which desperately needed labour and settlers – and an ideal way of easing the burden of Britain's poor and homeless children.

It had all been started by an Englishwoman named Maria Susan Rye, a zealous, determined character who worked among the poor people of London. In 1868 she went to Canada and bought an old jail on the outskirts of a small town called Niagara-on-the-Lake, which lay at the mouth of the River Niagara at Lake Ontario. The jail was gutted and refurbished, and in October 1869 Maria Rye took sixty-eight children from Liverpool and London to Montreal on the SS *Hibernian*. The children, from the workhouses of London and an industrial school in Liverpool, were of all ages, the youngest (nine and under) bound for adoption, and the older ones to be indentured as farm hands or domestics.

Maria Rye was followed just a few months later by Annie Macpherson, the tireless Scots philanthropist who went to work in London in 1865 and who encouraged William Quarrier to go ahead with his plan for a children's Home in Renfrew Lane in Glasgow. She, like Barnardo after her, saw emigration as a positive solution to the problem of London's overcrowded, poverty-ridden streets. She proclaimed her conviction in a stirring pamphlet written in 1869:

> We who labour here are tired of relieving misery from hand to mouth, and also heartsick of seeing hundreds of families pining away for want of work, when over on the shores of Ontario the cry is heard, 'Come over and we will help you'...We are waiting to seek out the worthy not yet on the parish list, but who soon must be; we will see to their being properly started on the Canadian shores if you will give us the power to make a golden bridge across the Atlantic.

In the spring of 1870 Annie Macpherson took a hundred boys from her own rescue homes, the workhouses and the reformatories in London, to Ontario. There the townspeople of Belleville, a town on Lake Ontario, gave her a large house, rent-free, called Marchmont, to which she could send children for distribution to farms and homesteads throughout the province. As the work expanded and Annie Macpherson brought more and more children, she acquired other such homes all over Ontario. The golden bridge was now well and truly opened for traffic. Nearly

100,000 children from all over Britain would cross it during the period from 1870 to the early 1930s – more than 30,000 of them sent by Thomas Barnardo alone.

Dr Barnardo's first party of fifty-one boys made the journey to Canada in 1882. By that time William Quarrier had been sending children for ten years. From the first he recognised emigration as an important factor in his work for Scotland's orphans, and when he met Annie Macpherson they agreed that he would send the children from his Renfrew Lane Home to Canada under her auspices. For Quarrier, emigration was not just a convenient means of clearing Glasgow's streets of waifs and strays; of course it was clear that his Glasgow Homes had limited accommodation and training facilities for the children and that emigration was essential if more and more were to be rescued, but Quarrier also firmly believed that emigration was in the best interests of his children and that Canada was truly the land of opportunity, where boys and girls could make a good future for themselves in a new, eager country which needed them. His children would be following the route taken by thousands of pioneers and settlers before them, not least their Scottish ancestors. After the Jacobite Rebellion in 1745 and the break-up of the clan system, wave upon wave of Highlanders broke on the distant shores of eastern Canada. They settled in Quebec, Ontario, Cape Breton and right across to British Columbia, sharing the vast unexplored land with people from all over the world.

Ontario was by far the most popular province and it was to this area that Quarrier sent his first band of children on 2 July 1872. The group consisted of thirty-five boys from the Cessnock Home and twenty-nine other children from orphanages in Maryhill and Edinburgh, all under the charge of Quarrier's friend, the Rev. Stobo, and Miss Bryson, one of the teachers at Renfrew Lane. Their ship, the SS *St David*, was one of the Allan Line steamers, identified by their red, white and black funnels, which made regular voyages from Glasgow to Canada and America. On the morning of departure, Quarrier's boys were marched from Cessnock to the Broomielaw, their trunks going on ahead by horse and cart. At the dockside all was activity and bustle as people gathered to see off the ship, many of them friends and relatives of the children. Quarrier stood among the excited, chattering boys as their luggage was loaded onto the ship, each trunk stamped with the boy's initials and containing, among other things, one cloth and two linen suits, four shirts, four pairs of socks, a box of collars, writing material and a pair of strong boots. The cost of all this and a one-way passage to Quebec was just £10. Quarrier also provided his boys with one or two other items to kit them out for their new lives — a reference Bible, a copy of *Pilgrim's Progress* and a pocket knife. It was all good equipment for the young pioneer. At last, farewells were said, the ship's whistle on the great funnel sounded and the *St David* cast off.

Looking after sixty-four excited children of all ages for sixteen days in the middle of the Atlantic was not without its difficulties, and the Rev. Stobo's journal is full of vivid little details of life on board:

> It is difficult to prevent things going astray on board ship, and some people allow things strange to them to stick to them, to others' loss and discomfort …Of course, boys cannot be made girls, they will be boisterous and romping, and full of fun, and it's no use trying to coop them up in a corner.

The ship steamed up the St Lawrence River on 17 July and arrived in Quebec at noon the following day. From there the whole party went by train to Montreal and then east to one of Annie Macpherson's distribution homes in the little township of Knowlton. Brome Hall, which was a converted public house, was run by a Miss Barbour, and the Rev. Stobo stayed just long enough to hand over into her care some of his charges to be sent to homes in this south-eastern corner of Quebec. Then he was off again, this time west to Annie Macpherson's main home, Marchmont, in Belleville. This home was later put in the charge of one of Annie Macpherson's closest friends, Ellen Agnes Bilbrough, and used exclusively for Quarrier's children until 1887, when Quarrier built a brand-new home in Brockville a little further up the St Lawrence river. Marchmont home distributed children all over central Canada and to farmsteads for 200 miles in all directions, some of them very isolated.

The Rev. Stobo's last port of call was the town of Galt, named after the Scottish novelist John Galt,* which lay south-west of Lake Ontario.

---

* John Galt's (1779–1839) best-known novel was *The Annals of the Parish*. He went to Canada himself in 1826, founded the town of Guelph and played a prominent part in organising immigration there. He went bankrupt and returned to Britain in 1829.

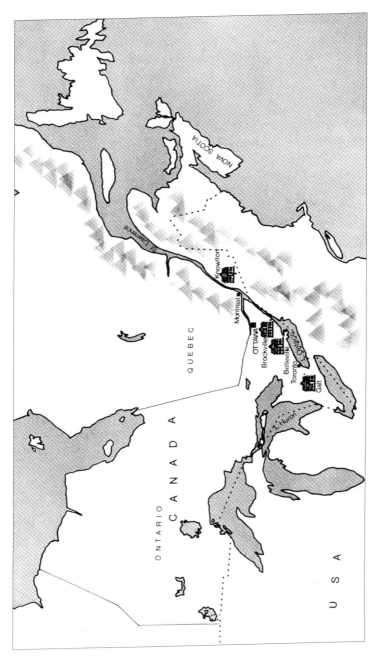

Map showing the locations of the Distribution Homes for the children sent to Canada from the Orphan Homes of Scotland

He delivered more children there, this time to Blair Athole, a farm just outside the town which served as another of Annie Macpherson's distribution homes. In all, the Rev. Stobo spent six weeks in Canada and travelled more than 3,500 miles by pony-trap, wagon and train, delivering his precious cargo of children. He accompanied some of them all the way to their new homes in outlying districts and this often meant long, uncomfortable journeys on poor roads.

Ontario in the 1870s was, like most of the rest of Canada, a rural province. Of a population of 3,500,000 in Canada in 1871, only about 12 per cent lived in cities and towns, and only twenty towns had more than 5,000 inhabitants. Montreal, with 107,000 inhabitants, Quebec with 60,000 and Toronto with 57,000 were the three most concentrated areas of population in the entire country. And what of the vast open countryside that was the rest of Canada? Nothing could have been more different to the eyes and experience of a child born and raised on the dirty, crowded streets of nineteenth-century Glasgow. To the children Quarrier sent over to Canada, Ontario would have been an almost unrecognisable world: small hamlets and tiny communities spread over empty miles instead of high tenements stacked against one another and lining the streets; acres of wheat fields and miles of grasslands instead of teeming thoroughfares. A child sent to a remote farm in Ontario might be many miles from the nearest neighbour and would certainly have to traverse a considerable distance to attend school. The only regular social gathering he or she would encounter would probably be weekly church attendance.

Everything must have looked different, smelt different and sounded different. Vast blue skies and burning sun in the summer months, and then sub-zero winter temperatures and quantities of snow such as were never seen in the Gallowgate. Many a child would have encountered a cow for the first time in his life – and how strange the farm with all its animals and open spaces would smell! And how would the wind rushing across the fields and through the trees sound to a young girl in bed at night who had spent most of her life amid the bustle and clamour of Glasgow's streets?

However unfamiliar and strange Canada was to these girls and boys, they would have had little time to cry. They were there to work; those under twelve were adopted and worked as part of the family

MISS BILBROUGH'S HOME, CANADA.

Marchmont Home, Belleville, Ontario, 24th Oct., 1879.

DEAR FRIENDS,—It is with feelings of deep gratitude, I sit down to write my usual contribution to our Annual Report, knowing how much interest is taken by you in the well doing of the children sent out from Scotland.

Reproduced from the 1879 Narrative of Facts

for their board and keep; the older children were indentured and paid a small wage which went into a savings account to be given to them when they left their employer. In the months before a party of children arrived, those in charge at the Canadian end (Miss Bilbrough and later Quarrier's daughter, Agnes, and her husband, James Burges) advertised through churches, in local newspapers and Christian and missionary circles, for those farmers either interested in adopting a 'Scotch child' or taking one on as a farm hand. Agnes Bilbrough described in her booklet *British Children in Canadian Homes* the pains which were taken to make sure of the suitability of each home, but the process merely seems to have involved talking to the applicant, asking round the neighbours and gaining a good word from the local minister. It appears from Miss Bilbrough's account that a farmer who arrived on the doorstep to pick out a child simply needed to produce a reference, sign a few papers and take the child away. But whatever the shortcomings in the selection of homes, Agnes Bilbrough did keep a careful note of each child and where he or she went. All the children were registered and every applicant had to sign a Form of Indenture for a child of twelve or over:

> This indenture made this .... day of ....(Pursuant to Order in Council bearing the date 9th December, 1879, authorising Marchmont Home to exercise the powers granted under sec. 19 of cap. 135, RSO) is entered into between Ellen Agnes Bilbrough, Marchmont, guardian of .... and Mr .... respecting .... To receive 4 dollars per month for the first year, increasing annually. To attend Church and Sunday School regularly. Also day school four months in the year. Should it be necessary in any case for the child to be returned to the Home, notice of this must be sent a fortnight beforehand. The clothes must also be sent back in good condition, and the same number. Employers are requested to see that the children write occasionally to their friends; also that they communicate with us in the event of sickness. An accurate account to be kept by employer of the wages spent in child's clothing etc. The account to be balanced each year, and said balance to be deposited in Savings Bank, or otherwise laid out to child's advantage. Persons taking these children cannot transfer them to others, but are at liberty to return them to the Home if they do not suit, while we, on our part, reserve the right of removing any child if we see fit, or on these conditions not being fulfilled.

Anyone who adopted a child under twelve had to sign a form along the same lines, but instead of wages the child was to receive 'good clothing and schooling and be treated as one of the family'.

Annual visits by representatives of the Home were really the only way to check that things were well with the child, that a boy or girl was not being ill-treated and that the limited terms of agreement were being carried out properly. Word of trouble, however, might travel along the grapevine of church circles and neighbours' conversations, and if the Home suspected anything was wrong they would send out the Visitor. The Visitor tried to do the job conscientiously but time, distance and numbers made it a very hard task. The numbers of children sent over from Quarrier's Homes in Glasgow increased steadily, especially after the opening of the homes at Bridge of Weir. Thirty-five boys were sent out in the first year (1872), sixty-six the following year, 103 in 1879 and in 1881 two separate parties – fifty boys in March and sixty-eight girls in May. After this, two parties were sent out every year and in 1885 there was even a third exodus – a total of 339 children went to Canada in that year alone. To cope with the rising numbers, in 1887 Quarrier bought a property to use as his new distribution Home, solely for his children, in a little town called Brockville. It was called Fairknowe Home and the remains of it still stand in the town today, part of an apartment block. The records of the 2,000 children already in the country were transferred to the new Home and Quarrier's daughter and her husband went out to run the operation.

They had a huge task. Quarrier's children were spread over a vast area that stretched from the eastern shores of Lake Huron right across to Montreal and beyond, and from Lake Ontario in the south to the borders of Quebec. James Burges' brother, Alexander, was Fairknowe's principal resident Visitor and he spent virtually the whole year trekking through the countryside to outlying farms, in all weathers, checking up on the children. His report of 1892, by which time his visiting roll listed some 3,000 names (although many of these would be grown-up Quarrier's boys and girls), gives some idea of the travelling involved:

> Last fall I drove as far west as Belleville, taking Wolfe Island, Amherst Island, and Prince Edward County on my way west, and visiting the northern part of the counties on my return. As the roads were heavy, it was anything but agreeable work. After New Year I went through all Western Ontario, getting back in time to meet the party of boys. During summer I got over a good deal of ground, although the weather was exceedingly warm, and we had a number of unusually severe storms . . . During the year we have visited over 2,000 of the children.

Generally, Fairknowe was well satisfied with its children and their new lives – the Burgeses always maintained that about 95 per cent of them did well and only a very small percentage ran off, or were a source of trouble or annoyance. (They didn't tend to write assessments of whether the children were happy or not, but one can speculate about the reasons why children 'ran off'.) Quarrier did not draw his children straight from reformatory schools or out of the poorhouse as did people like Maria Rye in England, and he insisted that they were not simply decanted from Glasgow's streets into the homesteads of Ontario but received training at home beforehand. In the early days this could not

Fairknowe Home, Brockville, which Quarrier built in 1887

have been much more than being cleaned up and taught a little reading and writing and some table manners, because Cessnock and Renfield Homes were really just transit homes – children would be admitted and packed off to Canada within months. However, once the Homes at Bridge of Weir were opened it was possible to train the children for longer periods and prepare them a little for their new lives. As far as he could help it, Quarrier did not send wild or unruly children or those likely to revert to street habits of stealing or roughness, and he believed he was supplying Canada with good future citizens.

Ironically, this was what aroused a degree of hostile criticism at home. Some sections of Scottish business and industry complained that such mass emigration of Scotland's young was draining the future labour market; Quarrier's confident reply was that it wasn't the labour market he was reducing but a future crime market of children abandoned to the streets, and that by taking them in at an early age, training them up and sending them to new lives in Canada, he was doing the poorhouse, the rate-payers, the citizens and the children a favour.

But the British emigration movement faced far more serious and disturbing criticism than this. Three years after Quarrier sent his first party of boys to Ontario, a report was published in England which exposed serious shortcomings in some of the British agencies for child emigration. The report was written by Andrew Doyle, a 65-year-old lawyer and former inspector for the London Poor Law Board. The Local Government Board, which had taken over the work of the Poor Law Board, decided in 1874 that an investigation should be made of the various British emigration bodies. The scheme had been running for five years now and the Board had supplied it with hundreds of children from England's workhouses and reformatories. They formed a considerable proportion of the 2,000-odd boys and girls now scattered across Canada from Nova Scotia to Manitoba. Rumours had reached the Board which caused anxiety about the welfare of some of the children and so, in spring 1874, they sent out Andrew Doyle to investigate.

His findings were far from reassuring. He spent six months travelling round the country, visiting first the distribution Homes of Maria Rye and Annie Macpherson and then as many of the children as he could. He questioned Miss Rye and Miss Macpherson and all their helpers, inquiring into everything from finances to the sleeping arrangements for the children coming into their Homes. And his conclusion was that, although both Maria Rye and Annie Macpherson were led by the best and most sincere motives, their respective organisations were badly run along the whole line, from the initial selection of children to their placing out in Canadian farms.

One of his main worries was that, in the choosing of the children from the workhouses, little or no distinction was made between paupers and waifs who were there through no fault of their own and the hardened so-called 'street arabs', many of them thieves and semi-criminals from an early age. Children were simply lifted from the workhouses, wrote Andrew Doyle, the good apples with the bad, and many a farmer ended up receiving an unruly thief for a farm hand, which lent discredit to the whole movement.

Andrew Doyle also criticised the forms of indenture which each applicant had to sign. These were not stringent enough to ensure the child's well-being, and prospective households were not inspected properly beforehand. On the subject of inspection and visiting, Doyle had his most hard-hitting remarks to make, though here he carefully distinguished between Annie Macpherson's operation and Maria Rye's. He was absolutely appalled by the lack of any proper supervision of Maria Rye's children once they had been taken off her hands. She didn't even keep records, so that she had no idea of what happened to most of them – they could have been ill-treated and left their guardian or employer, and she would have known nothing about it.

Doyle was less severe on Annie Macpherson and he had nothing but praise for Agnes Bilbrough. 'The liberal and unostentatious way', he wrote, 'in which that lady devotes the rare gifts with which she is endowed to the fulfilment of very onerous duties is beyond all praise'. He recognised that Annie Macpherson did have a system of visiting which was carried out as faithfully as possible, but it was imperfect; there were simply too many children, they were too far afield and one annual visit was not enough.

Amazingly, Andrew Doyle's report and his call for a much more carefully planned and regulated emigration system were almost totally ignored in Canada. It was widely reported in the British press and demands were made for a halt to the movement until things had been put right; but in Canada most people simply refused to believe the report, and the supporters of Maria Rye, who did not want to see their source of labour disappear, poured scorn on Doyle and his findings.

Some years later, though, public opinion in Canada began to change. Although farmers always remained in favour of the British children, the 1880s saw many Canadians turn against immigration. During the late 1870s and mid-1880s, Canada suffered periodic bouts of economic depression and the anxieties and frustrations of working men became focused, not unnaturally, on the foreign workforce flooding the country. British children became the target for much criticism and there was resentment from the Canadian Trades and Labour Council, led by the trade unionist D.J. O'Donaghue, who said that they were a source of cheap labour which deprived the Canadian working man of a job. In addition, the very occasional court case involving a 'Home boy' and (generally unfounded) stories of assaults by such boys on their masters fuelled fears that Canada was becoming the dumping ground for the depraved and criminal elements of Britain's slums. 'Canada wants increased population,' wrote the *Globe* in 1884, 'but she would not on that account thank any country for landing the inmates of its prisons and poorhouses on her shores.'

In 1896 the case of a Barnardo boy, George Green, fanned the flames of controversy still higher. This poor boy was found dead, and in the most appalling state of filth and disease, at the farm of Miss Helen Findlay in Owen Sound, Ontario. According to the coroner, the boy died as a result of neglect, starvation and violence. During the trial of Miss Findlay for manslaughter it emerged that she had often been seen by neighbours physically abusing George – kicking him, hitting him with the handle of an axe and poking him with a pitchfork. But what caused the greatest furore in the press, far more than the charges of assault (which Miss Findlay denied), were other medical reports on George Green which claimed that he was physically extremely defective, had bad eyesight and had been suffering from a tuberculosis-related condition. In fact, announced the doctors who performed the second autopsy, George was a weak physical specimen to start with.

The Canadian press leapt upon this revelation and set up a clamour of invective against the practice of sending such diseased young people to infect their country and declared that the case exposed once and for all the

The girls' party of 1897 at Fairknowe Home. William Quarrier and his wife are standing in the middle of the second row from the back

weakness of the medical examinations of the British children coming into the country. Nobody seemed to think it worthwhile pointing out that the case of George Green also indicated the chilling possibility of the abuse of other children abandoned to isolated farms and left to the mercy of their employers.

But one man did fear the possibility that there were many George Greens all over Canada. He was John Kelso, the founding President of the Toronto branch of the Children's Aid Society and the Superintendent of Neglected Children in Ontario. He prepared *A Special Report on the Immigration of British Children* in 1897 in which he urged the regulation of the work, the official inspection of all emigration organisations and the tightening-up of visiting and inspection of children.

By this time there were nearly 40,000 British children in Canada, and 28,945 of them were on farms in Ontario. The federal government of Ontario realised that something had to be done to improve and control the traffic in children, to protect them from possible cruelty and suffering and to safeguard Canada from an influx of undesirables. So in March 1897 Ontario passed an 'Act to Regulate the Immigration into Ontario of Certain Classes of Children', which was designed to place Homes children under official control from the moment they stepped off the boat until the age of eighteen. Each Home had to apply for a licence and keep an up-to-date account of the character, movements and habits of every child in its hands.

Thus Ontario tried to keep track of all the British children within its borders. But William Quarrier was very angry at the new legislation. *His* children had never been complained about or diseased, or in trouble with the law, so why should he have to submit to all this new red tape and officialdom? He saw the act as interfering with his work and could see no justification for it. What irritated him most of all was that his work, far from being criticised, had always been praised by the government in Ontario; John Kelso had always maintained that Quarrier's organisation was well-run, as had the Premier, Arthur Hardy, who wrote personally to Quarrier in 1897 to explain the need for the Act and to reiterate that it in no way reflected badly on Quarrier's work. But Quarrier would not be appeased. The letter only made the new law appear more unfair and unnecessary for his children and he would have none of it. He refused to see that there were very many other people involved in the matter who were not carrying out their work as conscientiously as he, and that this legislation was an attempt to protect *their* children. One-man show that he was, Quarrier would not see that there couldn't be one law for him and a different one for everyone else. He remained stubborn and uncooperative; if he couldn't send children to Ontario exactly as he had been sending them before, he just wouldn't send any more.

So that year at Bridge of Weir there was no sound of hammering in the workshops where the trunks for Canada were made; no one went round the cottages making up lists of young emigrants and no bookings were made with the Allan Line. It seemed that the gates of the Orphan Homes of Scotland would remain firmly shut in the direction of Canada. But they did open again – the traffic of Quarrier's children across the golden bridge was not over yet.

Chapter 6

The Little Emigrants

All his life, Peter Graham treasured the little wooden box he made in the carpentry shop at Bridge of Weir back in 1929, two years before he was sent out to Canada. He kept all sorts of precious things in it: the Bible given to him when he left Quarrier's Homes, an old change purse, his first shaving brush which he made from the bristles of a worn paintbrush, a photograph of some boys playing football at the Homes and a letter from an aunt, dated 1937. Peter, who died in 2002, aged eighty-eight, spent more than sixty-six years working and living in Ontario, but he never lost that unmistakable Scottish burr in his Canadian drawl. He was a Canadian citizen, and proud of it, but his Scottish roots were still important to him.

Peter was one of hundreds of men and women all over Canada who started life originally in the Orphan Homes at Bridge of Weir. He belonged to the generation which went out to Canada in the 1920s and '30s; but for every original emigrant there are thousands more who are descendants of Peter's generation and thousands more again who are descended from earlier waves of juvenile emigration. William Quarrier stopped sending children in 1897 after the passing of the Ontario Act, but emigration resumed in 1904, the year after the founder died. His daughters and his son-in-law, Pastor David Findlay, decided that the Act was not a hindrance, as Quarrier had obstinately maintained, and in fact afforded much better protection and safeguards for the children. The Act ensured that each child's new home would be

*William Quarrier on board ship with a party of girls bound for Canada
(reproduced from Urquhart's Life Story of William Quarrier)*

inspected at least once a year by an independent government official, as well as by representatives of the various emigration agencies. There were to be rigorous medical examinations for every child, instead of the cursory inspection on arrival in Canada. In later years, officials from the Canadian government interviewed prospective emigrants in their Home in Britain and no one who failed that test was allowed to go.

Efforts were also made to tighten up the regulations regarding the schooling of the children in Canada. Before 1897, potential employers and guardians had merely to promise that the child would attend school for a few months in the year, but the Canadian authorities gradually became stricter about this. Soon every child of school age had to attend school for the full nine months in the year – not just for a few months in the winter when there was less to do around the farm. This made farmers less willing to take on children under school age, since it meant an extra mouth to feed in return for only limited help with farm work.

Much had changed since the pioneering 1870s and 1880s when Quarrier first sent children to Ontario; farming was becoming a serious business in the rapidly expanding and increasingly mechanised Canada of the early 1900s, and farmers wanted as much return for their money as they could get. In 1909, the average age of the boys and girls from the Orphan Homes was 13.3 and 12.8 respectively and by 1912 the *Narrative of Facts* was reporting lessening demand for those under fourteen. This was in striking contrast to the pre-1897 situation. Earlier issues of the *Narrative of Facts* would often carry photographs of the girls and boys on board ship, all neatly posed in rows on deck, the tallest at the back and the tiny mites in front, peering uncertainly over their high collars and almost drowned in their starched frocks. In 1892 Quarrier had accompanied more than 120 children to Quebec; according to the shipping list, nearly half the children on that voyage were under eleven. Seven were eight-year-olds, ten were seven, and there were six six-year-olds and a little brother and sister of just five. Sending such young children was out of the question when emigration resumed in 1904; not only was there less demand for them, but there was still a good deal of opposition to the movement and people concerned for the welfare of the children, on both sides of the Atlantic, continued to press for stricter controls.

So things were rather different on the emigration front by the time Pastor Findlay decided it should be started again. But the same preparations had to be made at Bridge of Weir. For weeks before the twice-yearly departure of the children, the Homes were a hive of activity. There were lists of names to be drawn up, trunks to be built, medical tests to be passed. On the evening before departure a service was held in Mount Zion to say farewell to those who were leaving. As the chosen ones filed out of the church at the end of the service the other children sang to them:

> Don't forget the Orphan Homes of Scotland,
> Don't forget the dear friends here;
> Don't forget that Jesus Christ your Saviour
> Goes with thee to Canada.
>
> And remember we are still a-praying
> That your life will be good and true,
> And that you may find a blessing
> In the land you're going to.

The next morning children and adults lined Faith Avenue to wave off the young emigrants; and when news of their safe arrival in Canada eventually reached the Superintendent, the bells of Mount Zion rang out around the village. The terrible sinking of the *Titanic* on 14 April 1912 sent a thrill of horror and relief round the Homes – their party of boys had reached Halifax safely by the same route a few days before.

Parties of children continued to leave for Quebec and Halifax throughout the 1920s. Numbers were gradually decreasing, however, and there was continuing public concern about the young age of children going overseas. As a result, the British government ruled in 1924 that no child under fourteen could be sent to work in Canada. By the late 1920s, too, Canada was suffering badly under the Depression and became unwilling to continue to admit immigrants on the same scale as before. In 1933 Canada closed its ports to mass juvenile immigration and in the following year Fairknowe was sold. Small numbers of boys and girls still went out occasionally from Quarrier's to join brothers and sisters already in Canada, but by 1939 the outbreak of war finally halted the child traffic across the golden bridge. (Interestingly, British Columbia arranged to have child migration laws temporarily lifted

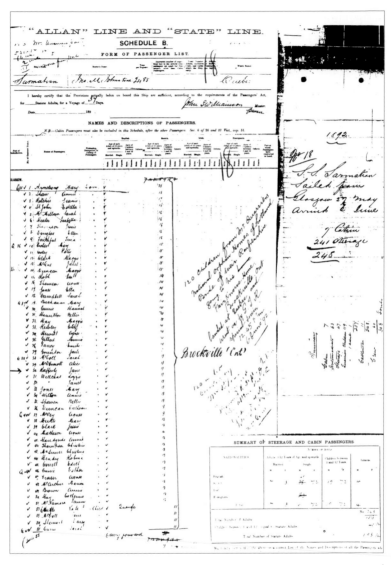

Extract from the passenger list of the SS Sarmatian (courtesy of the Public Archives of Canada). The top half of the hand-written section reads: 120 children from Mr Quarrier's National Orphan Homes of Scotland, Bridge of Weir, Renfrewshire, going to his Fairknowe Home, Brockville, Ont. Landed at Quebec and went on by G(?)IR special train 12.45 p.m. 6 June '92

in 1945 and for three years the Fairbridge Farm School organisation continued to send children from England out to a training farm on Vancouver Island.) Altogether, more than 7,000 had gone west from Bridge of Weir since that first party of boys who gathered at the Broomielaw in 1872.

James McCallum was one of the 7,000. He was sent to Canada when he was fifteen with a party of forty boys in April 1929. Despite all the regulations which had been introduced since Quarrier's time, and the good intentions of the Orphan Homes in sending children to new lives in Canada, it's only when you read the accounts of the emigrants themselves that you get a real sense of just how overwhelming and potentially grim the experience was. Life in Canada could turn out to be a nightmare, or it could be a fine chance for a better future, and there was nothing a young boy or girl could do to influence that. And even in the 1920s, as James McCallum's account shows, former Boys' and Girls' recollections reveal a worrying casualness about how they were prepared for emigration.

I was asked if I wanted to go to Canada but I cannot remember by whom, and my answer 'yes' was just an impulse, as up to that moment I had not dreamed of going anywhere, especially Canada.

There were no preparations for us prior to departure. No lectures, talks or anything that would prepare us for a new and strange life in Canada; but there was an interview with two officials of the Canadian Department of Immigration.

These interviews were conducted separately and privately for each boy, and we were asked questions of general knowledge.

The Orphan Homes owned two buses, one large and one small, and we were taken to the ship in the big bus. It was the custom for all boys and girls to line the road leading to the main gates and cheer us on our way. I can remember leaning out of the bus window trying to spot my sister in the crowd and screaming her name so that she would notice me. As we drove out of the gates I had a lump in my throat that had nothing to do with the Orphan Homes. It was for this little ten-year-old girl whom I suddenly realised I was leaving behind, possibly never to see again.

When I was sent out to my first farm I remember getting off the train at Lansdowne, Ontario, and waiting to be picked up. Mr Bradley arrived in a spring wagon drawn by two horses and his first words to me were, 'You're not very big, are you?'

In April in Canada, the frost is coming out of the ground and at that time there were no paved roads around that district, so everything was mud

*A typical Canadian farmstead to which British Homes children were
so often sent (reproduced by courtesy of Barnardo's)*

and the first thing I had to buy out of my wages was a pair of knee-high
rubber boots.

I was to get ten dollars per month in the summer and five dollars in the
winter months; however, up to that time I had never seen a cow milked and
could not have been of much use to him in the beginning.

I was very well treated by this man and his wife (they were not long
married) and one of my jobs on Monday morning was to turn the crank of
the washing machine for Mrs Bradley.

Learning how to harness horses, and the names of the various parts of
the harness, was confusing. The horses seemed like giants to me and a horse

is very quick to spot a greenhorn and take advantage. However, I learned quickly and in May, under supervision of my boss, I was working the horses in the field, preparing for spring planting.

The first summer in Canada was a lonely experience for me. I don't think I spent five cents out of my wages, except for clothes. There was nowhere to go and no way for me to get there if there had been.

We arose about 4.30 a.m. and worked as long as it was daylight, usually about 9 p.m. It was the custom for all farmers to work such hours. Any farmer who did not would have been thought to be very lazy by his neighbours, and no farmer wanted such a stigma attached to him. Of course, they were atrocious hours for a young boy to work, but it was usual for the time and nobody thought there was anything wrong.

Hundreds and hundreds of boys and girls like James McCallum began their careers in Canada in this way on the farmlands of eastern Ontario. It was a hard, uncompromising life; the children worked long hours in all weathers, learnt quickly and grew up even faster. From the age of fourteen, when they received wages, boys worked from 4 a.m. or 5 a.m. in the summer until nightfall; in winter the hours were shorter but it often meant working in freezing temperatures and wild conditions. Wages were low and, although board and lodging were included, the boys and girls were expected to buy their own clothes and other necessities. The children were cheap labour, but they were completely untrained and, especially during the Depression years, infinitely better off than so many people who had no job and hardly enough money to buy bread.

The boys did everything from felling trees to milking cows; they worked in the fields and drove the horses; during the harvest they spent back-breaking hours binding the corn into stooks and hauling the sheaves to the barns to be threshed. They had to learn everything from scratch. Peter Graham remembers how the farmer's sons used to laugh at him because he had such difficulty pitch-forking the corn on to the back of the wagon. He was seventeen but small for his age and the corn stalks were 8 to 10 feet long:

I would always have one foot at the top end and I'd be wondering why I couldn't get it up onto the wagon because I was standing on it because I was so small! And they used to tease me something awful about that. But I got so's that I thought, 'Boy, you'll never tease me for ever', and I got as good as any of them.

These boys and girls needed great determination to overcome the severe challenges of life on an Ontario farm in the early part of the century. Joan MacIntosh's father was only ten when he arrived in Canada in 1903:

> Late one autumn, having grown out of his only pair of boots and unable to procure replacements until enough money was accumulated, my father was obliged to perform three weeks of chores in bare feet. At that time of year Canadian weather is ranging from 32°F to 0°F, with frost covering the ground and ice forming overnight in puddles. Each morning Father would race from house to barn where, upon arrival, he would determine which was the freshest (and warmest) cow droppings. He would then warm his feet by standing in that 'cow pie' as long as possible and hoping that another would become available soon. To my mind, this truly emphasizes the type of hardship at least some of the Home children encountered in Canada. It should be remembered, however, that many Canadian children may have been subjected to the same desperate situation.

Girls, too, were expected to help around the farm; in addition to housework, cooking, cleaning and looking after any children, many girls worked in the fields and tended the animals. Joan Scott went to Canada in 1910 and was adopted by a family near Brockville. Her adoptive mother was a widow, which meant there was a tremendous amount of farm work for the women of the household to do. Joan milked the cows, cleaned the stables, pitched hay, helped with the ploughing and harrowing, scrubbed floors and looked after the house. Elsie Barker also remembered the farm work. She was ten when she arrived in Ontario in 1913, and her first job was to go out and collect the cows for milking at six o'clock in the morning. She had no shoes and had to race across the cold ground in her bare feet; one morning she had to run even faster because she was chased all the way by the bull! Elsie later laughed about how strange and foreign she found everything on the farm but, at the time, the culture shock for the Home children must have been overwhelming.

Hugh Blair went to Canada in 1930 at the age of sixteen. He recalled that when he arrived in Quebec he wanted to go straight back home because everyone was speaking French and he thought he'd been sent to the ends of the earth. Coming to Canada had seemed like an adventure to a teenage boy who just wanted to get out of Bridge of

A Home boy learning to handle a plough
(reproduced by courtesy of the Public Archives of Canada)

Weir. However, after eleven days at sea, a two-day journey by train from Quebec through to Brockville and another train ride north to Stittsville where the farmer met him in a Model T Ford truck, Hugh was completely disorientated:

> We got my trunk into his truck and we started in from Stittsville and, oh my God, there was nothing! No houses anywhere for about the first three miles, then you hit good farmland . . . and I'm coming through this and I'm thinking, 'Where am I going? Am I going right into the bush? Will I ever get out of here?'

As soon as they got to the farm, Hugh was introduced to the rest of the family and then it was straight out into the barn where he was confronted by the sight of fifty-five cows standing in a line waiting to be milked:

> I thought to myself, 'What in the blessed name of goodness do I do with these!' The closest I'd ever been to a cow was seeing one in a field in Glasgow. I couldn't milk a cow, I didn't know what to do! [The farmer] told me, 'Just wait till we ask you'. He was a very good man that way.

Hugh was fortunate that he landed with a farmer who had taken Home boys before and who understood how unskilled and uninformed he would be. For the first month Hugh said he was no use at all as a farm hand, but the farmer was patient and kind and gradually Hugh became more skilled and was able to do many chores: hoeing, gardening, cleaning the cattle, milking the cows (it took him six months to learn that) and driving the tractor. Hugh reckoned it took about six to eight months before he was completely confident in his work and did not need anyone to tell him what to do.

Learning farm work was only half the battle, though. Frank Moir, who went to Canada in 1938, recalled being left alone all day to weed a sugarbeet field and crying with the sheer loneliness of it and with the ache of homesickness for Bridge of Weir and the brothers he had left there. These boys and girls from Quarrier's had spent most of their lives in an institution, a place where their lives were regulated, organised and controlled, where they were educated and where they socialised; they knew very little beyond the gates of the Homes and were certainly completely unprepared for their lives in Canada. A few general knowledge questions from a Canadian immigration official and perhaps a lesson at school on Canadian history and climate could never have equipped them for life in a foreign country, on their own, often on a farm miles from their nearest neighbour, without the support of the people with whom they had grown up.

Hugh Blair remembered Sundays, when there were fewer chores to be done, as the worst days for homesickness:

> I don't think there's any feeling like it, homesickness. If you haven't experienced it you wouldn't know it. It's so overpowering. I remember one Sunday feeling it so bad that I went out walking. Where I was going to I have no idea, but I was walking towards the station where I had got off the train. I must have walked about three miles and I was still about two miles from that station when I suddenly realised the futility of what I was doing, and I came back . . . I can remember lying in bed and I'd be thinking about the park where I used to play soccer, back in the Home, and the River Gryffe and walking across the bridge and if I could just get back and walk in these old familiar haunts again, wouldn't it be so great? . . . I would say it'd be six months before that only happened occasionally.

One of the hardest things to adjust to in their new lives in Canada was being separated from siblings. Quarrier's did try to place brothers and sisters together or in the same area but it was by no means automatic; and if only one brother or sister went to Canada, leaving others behind, they might never see one another again. Brothers and sisters were separated into girls' and boys' cottages when they went into the Orphan Homes – a practice which didn't stop until the 1960s – but at least they could see one another at school and in the evenings. Once there was an ocean between them, the chances of ever seeing one another again were slim.

Frank Moir left behind his younger brother, Alfred, when he went to Canada in 1938. Another brother, Robert, had already left the Homes, and there were four other brothers still living at home in Perth with their widowed father. Frank corresponded with Alfred, but never saw him again. He met up with one or two other brothers during the war, but after that he never knew if he had brothers still living.

William Beresford went to Canada in 1920, leaving his young brother behind. After the first years he wrote to the Homes at Bridge of Weir, saying, 'It's real lonesome out here', and asking if his brother

THREE BROTHERS IN CANADA.
The eldest, sent to Canada in 1892, forwarded money to take out his two brothers.

This photograph and caption appeared in the 1901 Narrative of Facts

could come over to join him. His brother, however, did not want to leave Scotland and, although the boys kept in touch, they remained on opposite sides of the Atlantic.

Ellen Buck travelled to Canada with her sister in 1911 but they were placed on different farms. Life was hard for a twelve-year-old child:

Quarrier had a home in Brockville where we were taken after landing, where we spent a few days. Jessie and I left at the same time, but she left the train before I did which upset me very much.

I was met at the station by Mr Andrew Pritchard. We had quite a long drive to his farm at Dunrobin. Mrs Pritchard and their sons were all at home. It was a frightening experience for a shy twelve-year-old; I couldn't understand why they should laugh at my Scottish tongue ...

I got very little time to go to school. I was soon able to go for the cows, and help to milk, to feed chickens, pigs and calves. The Pritchards had a big farm with a large garden; many a time I cried with cold hands and broken nails, picking up turnips, of which we had many loads. The cattle were fed turnips once a day and we had to put the turnips through a chopper ...

I was glad when my sister Jessie was moved closer to where I was. It was five miles away. I would visit her on Sunday and ran back the five miles to help milk the cows.

But though the work was hard, generally the children were well fed, clothed and housed. Plenty of milk, butter and eggs and three solid meals a day seems to have been the normal fare for most of them. Thomas Alexander lived in the Orphan Homes until 1945 and went to Canada on his own after seeing a poster in a railway station in Ayr, advertising the 'land of opportunity'. One of the things which impressed him most when he got his first job on a farm was that the hired man had his meals with his employer, something he had not experienced very often when he worked on farms in Scotland.

Generally the girls and boys had their own room in the farmhouse. Sometimes a boy would share a room with his employer or the son of the house, or a girl might share with the daughter. The farmhouses tended to be two-storey brick buildings with outside sanitation, although conditions varied according to how isolated the farm was.

Catherine Wardle arrived in Ontario in 1928 and got rather a shock when she reached her new farm some miles from Ottawa and discovered how basic the amenities were:

> When we arrived at the farm I was shown my bedroom upstairs. When we came down I asked Mrs Leach where the lavatory was. She took me outside and told me it was just round the corner. I was rather shocked when I saw it. I'd never seen anything like that before. I expected to see a flush toilet. But this was country living. I remember writing to my mother and telling her how backward they were in Canada.
>
> There was a hand pump in the kitchen so we would wash the dishes, but had to heat the water on the wood stove and if one wanted a bath one just took some warm water upstairs to the bedroom and filled the basin and had a sponge bath. A basin and jug were kept in the room.
>
> There was no electricity then and we used oil lamps.

Most of the men and women who look back on their early days in Canada tend not to want to dwell on the bad times and the difficulties. Just getting on with it was what saw them through and that is what they had been trained to do at home in Bridge of Weir. Life back in Scotland had been disciplined and spartan and, in the end, perhaps that was the best training for life in Canada. They had been brought up in the Homes to be grateful for what they had, to be self-reliant, to work hard and not complain, to do as they were told and to make something of themselves; these were indeed the qualities they needed in Canada. Life for the Homes children was certainly without any frills or concessions to age and inexperience, and most of them got through by adapting as best they could. Some, however, had to endure the added burden of ill-treatment. Compared to some other big organisations which sent children out to remote farms, Quarrier's had a good record, but it was by no means perfect and some children did endure cruelty and harsh treatment at the hands of their employers and guardians. Most cases date from the earlier years before tougher controls were imposed, but potentially every child was at risk, whether they went out in the 1890s or the 1920s. The children were very vulnerable and completely at the mercy of the families with whom they were placed. They were dependent upon the distribution homes to find them good families and to visit them regularly to make sure things were all right. If these things were not properly attended to, the consequences for the child could be harsh.

Mrs Wallace Smith's mother and aunt went to Ontario in 1889; her aunt, Katie, ended up with a family who treated her very badly:

> My Aunt Katie could not eat rice pudding with raisins, but she was told she had to eat it. That night she vomited in her bed. For this she was put in solitary confinement in the cold for three days, then brought out and severely whipped. This she knew was going to happen all the while she was in confinement.

Rose Loughheed's mother and aunt were also sent to Canada in the nineteenth century. Her aunt, Grace, went to a farm in a little place called Greenfield, in Ontario. She was only eight, separated from her sister and without anyone to turn to:

> The farmer drank excessively and sometimes beat her. Her teeth were very bad and she was overweight. One day at school she became hysterical. She was removed from that farm and sent to another where she received medical and dental treatment and was kindly treated.

It was this kind of situation, arising from poor selection and inspection of homes, which the *Glasgow Herald* was concerned about as early as

1883. In an editorial in February of that year the newspaper strongly criticised the lack of information available to the British public about just what went on at the Canadian end of juvenile emigration:

> We want to know, for example, what is done for the very young children who are sent out – whether they receive the education which they would be compelled to receive in this country if they remained here; whether at the most tender years they are not hired out to struggling farmers; whether they are treated with ordinary fairness, not to speak of ordinary humanity? ... Our Government have allowed this irresponsible deportation of the unprotected to go on without in any way troubling themselves about it.

The 1897 Act did make improvements, and Fairknowe Home tried to be diligent in its choice and inspection of homes but even so, with only one or, at most, two visits from their representatives in a year, there was always the chance that a child could be mistreated. Some were fortunate in finding very good homes. Harry Braebner, for instance, went to work for a family in Ontario in 1920 when he was fifteen. He worked on their farm for three years, kept in touch with the people and wrote of them that they were 'my first real family'. Hugh Blair was taken immediately into the bosom of his family, the Caldwells, and wrote later that 'I had come to the best place in the world to work for a real gentleman'. Peter Graham said he was well treated and he remembers the family at his first farm with affection; he called the farmer's wife 'mother' – 'she was the only mother I knew, so to me she was mother'.

David Donaldson, who went to Canada in 1927 at the age of sixteen, was not so lucky, either with the farms he worked at or with support from the Homes' authorities. He ran away from his first farm because they locked the door on him at nine o'clock at night, leaving him to sleep in the barn. He found a job at another farm but said:

> That was walking out of the frying pan into the fire. The farmer kicked me, punched me, broke a couple of ribs on me. The least thing I done wrong – maybe I didn't even know what I was doing – he got me down and kicked me ... I wrote to the Fairknowe Home and told them how I was being used. And they said, 'Oh, you're lying, Davie. These are good church people.' And from that day to this I've had very little use for 'good church people'.

In general, however, the majority of children from Bridge of Weir seem to have got by alright in their new homes. They might not have been happy, but they adapted to their new lives as best they could, endured the difficult times and, as they gradually became used to their new surroundings and more confident in an alien environment, they could begin to enjoy the novelty of being in a new country. Archie Aitken, who went to Canada in 1931, remembered his delight at seeing his first flock of young turkeys scurrying down the road one evening as he was returning home from the milking.

Catherine Wardle discovered how little she knew about the flora of Canadian farms:

> One day in the spring I saw this lovely yellow flower by the fence. I picked it and set it in a dish on the kitchen table. When Mrs Leach came into the room and saw this beauty she asked me where I had got it. I said, 'By the fence'. 'Well,' she said, 'if you had left it there, it would have turned into a pumpkin.' Was my face red!

Frank Moir had warm memories of the country store in those small Ontario hamlets:

> I enjoyed the fellowship, going to the country store in the evening, watching labourers sitting round the pot-bellied stove, chewing tobacco, and being fascinated at how they'd spit – ping – and hit the stove each time. That was a memory that stayed with me. I also learned how to ice skate, down with my friends at the river. I used to fall down a lot at first, but they'd get me up again.

Jimmie Drysdale arrived at his first farm in 1928. He remembered the food and the weather vividly:

> We always had oatmeal porridge in the morning. But the way they had it – they'd put brown sugar on the porridge. They wondered why I didn't put sugar on. It was funny, you know, just the difference in the people. When I first came to Canada, the breakfast drink was cocoa, but we got out of that and coffee came in. We didn't buy a pickle or a thing in the stores – it was all homemade, yessir. And I remember they used to kill a pig in the fall and put it in a barrel and salt it. And our neighbour used to give us beef and what was left come March or so, we'd just go out and cut a piece off and take it in, because the weather was colder then – it stayed cold all winter, it wouldn't thaw back. So we'd just go out and cut a piece, put it in a roast pan, take a piece of the salt pork and put it in with the beef . . . that was good . . . In the wintertime, it was good, you had to use a horse and sleigh all the time – the roads weren't ploughed. And you had to take the milk to the factory on the

sleigh and you'd have to put all the blankets and quilts you could over the milk to keep it from freezing. And you'd walk along beside the sleigh and you'd have your little gum rubbers on your feet and your feet would freeze inside them and you'd have to kick to keep your feet warm. The rubber was like a stick of wood on your feet and then later they came out with the insulated ones.

It took Hugh Blair about a year to begin to feel at home in Canada and slowly, slowly he became part of a community; he looked back on these times with real affection:

In those days you traded help for such things as threshing, corn cutting and wood sawing, and they were real affairs. The one farm wife trying to outdo the other by the meals they served up to the twenty or so men that sat down to dinner and supper. There were no coffee breaks but during the half hour that we sat around waiting for our dinner to digest, we swapped tales, traded life histories and in general got to know one another. I didn't like the suit I had come over with. It was made of that durable tweed that is now so fashionable and so expensive. When I finally had saved enough money to buy a blue serge suit I started to go to church, joined the choir and went to all sorts of things connected with the sociability of church life. Back then there were Sunday School picnics, choir and male quartet practices, rehearsing for plays to raise money, church suppers for the same reason, 17 March concerts, Christmas concerts beside the house parties and card parties. I can still hear them shouting, 'You're euchered!', scolding their partners for not playing this card or that card, their impatience with those who deliberated too long.

Hugh Blair gradually built a life in the community he'd come to and could say with conviction, at the end of his life (he died in January 1999), 'I came to the best country in the world'.

Letters and life stories from other people like Hugh suggest that most Quarrier's men and women eventually felt the same; they embraced their new country and became Canadian citizens by law and in spirit. But it was often very hard in the start because, like it or not, they were outsiders and incomers. Catherine Wardle never forgot the conversation she overheard when she had only been in Canada a few days:

The first Sunday I was at the farm I went to church with Mrs Leach and her son. Just behind us I heard two girls whispering; one was asking, 'Who's she?' The other girl said, 'She's just one of these Home girls' . . . I really felt hurt when I heard this and I heard it quite often —'Oh, she's one of those Home girls'.

The so-called Home Children were different; they were foreigners, orphans. They stood out because they were alone, they spoke differently, they were often small for their age, they had no family and they came from institutions. None of this meant that the Quarrier's Home Children were treated badly, but they were sometimes regarded as second-class citizens and, indeed, many of them felt insecure because of their origins and the fact that they came from an orphanage.

Peter Graham, who went to Canada in 1931, told of meeting an elderly woman at a public auction in the 1990s; she had heard him talking and asked him if he was Scottish. Peter said he was, and she asked, 'Where from?' He said, 'From the Quarrier Home.' 'You, too?' she replied. 'You know,' she whispered, 'I didn't want to speak to you in front of my son. He doesn't know I'm from the Home. My husband doesn't know anything about it.' 'Why is that?' Peter asked. 'Oh,' she said, 'I felt ashamed.'

Peter did not feel that way. He was proud of his Scottish origins in Quarrier's and proud of the life he made for himself in Canada. But he understood how some people found it more difficult to talk about their background and simply locked their past away, because he felt the isolation keenly when he first arrived:

> There was a kind of stigma attached to us. We were orphans, hired men attached to the farm, we were emigrants, so we felt we were lower-class. Some people were very receptive to us and others were not . . . You see, we were never asked any questions, none of the farmers ever asked me about the Home or where I'd been before the Home or what relatives I had – there were no questions ever asked. So we drew within ourselves . . . that was the way with a lot of us, we kept it within ourselves.

Between 1872 and end of the 1930s more than 7,000 children went overseas from Quarrier's to new lives in Canada. They were only a drop in the ocean out of the total of nearly 100,000 children sent by a host of other charitable organisations, orphanages and religious foundations all over Britain. They made an enormous contribution to the building and development of Canada and that contribution is slowly being recognised, even if some Home Children themselves do not speak of it, or find it too painful. The children, grandchildren and great-grandchildren of the original Quarrier's emigrants are proud of the achievements of their antecedents and they are intensely curious about the lives they led in Canada and in Scotland; they are tireless in their researches to uncover their family roots, and driven by a desire to understand things sometimes not spoken about; they want to discover what made their mothers, fathers, grandparents, aunts and uncles the people they were; and they want to tell their stories. And there are thousands upon thousands of stories to be told.

Thomas Duncan, who went to Canada at the age of eleven with his sister, Elizabeth, and his niece, Helen, writes with pride of the way brother and sister succeeded in building lives for themselves. They were placed with families near one another and Elizabeth continually supported Thomas in his schooling. She used her small wages to buy the books and clothes he needed for High School, and even gave him the money she had been saving up to buy a sewing machine for herself. Thomas managed to go to university, encouraged and helped through it all by his sister; eventually the young Scots boy who had come from an orphanage to work on a farm in Ontario ended up as Professor Emeritus of Greek at Washington University in Missouri, USA.

Peggy Jefferson's grandmother, Jane Rafferty, went to Canada from Quarrier's in 1892 but Peggy knew nothing about her background because 'it was never talked about in our house'. Peggy spent months researching Jane's story, getting hold of her records at Quarriers, trying to find out where she went in Ontario and what kind of life she led. When she found Jane's name on the ship's passenger list she cried, 'because I had found her. After all this time, I had found her'.

Beverly Kearns, whose mother was from Quarrier's, believes that the story of Scotland's little emigrants should be shouted from the rooftops throughout Canada:

> I feel very strongly that this country should appreciate what the Home children did for this country. And it's not known . . . when I started talking to people I found they knew nothing of the child migration programme, and this makes me very angry. Our government owes it to them at least to acknowledge that these children came. Many of them got a good home, but the thing was that they went out from these farms with not many skills and they created families who contributed to society and yet, in this country, the general public doesn't know about the Home children.

As the years go by, there are fewer and fewer original emigrants still alive to tell their stories, but the thousands of descendants of the Quarrier's emigrants will ensure that Canada – and Scotland – do not forget them. The 7,000 took nothing with them to Canada save a trunk of clothes and an education. They endured the loneliness, the stigma and, sometimes, the ill-treatment; they worked hard and saved hard, started families and made lives for themselves across the length and breadth of that vast country.

James McCallum counted himself among those who built much out of so little:

> Canada was fortunate indeed to receive such future citizens; it was Scotland's loss that they were sent away.

Chapter 7

The Pioneer

The last few years of William Quarrier's life were spent as industriously and enthusiastically as ever. Far from being content to sit back and keep a paternal eye on the activities of the Orphan Homes and the City Home and Mission, Quarrier wanted to extend and diversify his work. While hundreds of children made the journey across the Atlantic to far-off places, he too was exploring new horizons at his home in Bridge of Weir.

It was typical of Quarrier that he should focus his attention on, and direct his energies towards, an area of contemporary concern. When he formed his Shoe-black Brigade and opened his first children's homes, Glasgow's pauper children were a scandal of the day. His many years' experience of the dreadful physical condition of the children he had helped now galvanised Quarrier into action against another scourge of the nineteenth century – tuberculosis.

Anyone who has ever read a Victorian novel will have come across the frail consumptive heroine, like Helen Burns in *Jane Eyre*, who grows weaker and thinner with coughing as each day passes. Quarrier encountered many young boys already debilitated by the disease in his Industrial Brigades, and each day he admitted children to his Homes who had lost one or both parents through its ravages.

Tuberculosis was a killer in nineteenth-century Britain. The disease took a terrible toll in Glasgow and the statistics make grim reading. In the period from 1855 to 1864 it was responsible for 13 per cent

*This dramatic sketch highlighting the unhealthy conditions in Glasgow houses
appeared in the Bee magazine of 7 October 1874
(reproduced by courtesy of The Mitchell Library)*

of the total death rate in the city; in 1875, together with bronchitis, it accounted for 47 per cent of all deaths. Tuberculosis was just one of the many diseases which spread easily in a city notorious for its overcrowding, bad housing and poor sanitation. From the early years of the century until the 1870s, Glasgow regularly fell victim to all kinds of epidemics: typhus raged in the city for a year in 1818 and broke out again in the 1820s and 1830s, and 3,000 died within the first ten months of a cholera epidemic in 1832. And both diseases struck again and again throughout the city during the middle decades of the nineteenth century.

People did gradually become aware of the importance of factors such as proper sanitation for preventing the occurrence and spread of disease, and by the second half of the century measures were being taken to ensure better public health. Fresh water was piped to the city from Loch Katrine in 1859; Glasgow appointed its first Medical Officer of Health, Dr William Gairdner, in 1863 (a year after Edinburgh appointed their first one, Dr Littlejohn), and four years later the first Public Health (Scotland) Act was passed.

These and other measures, like better housing, contributed to the decrease in the number of deaths from tuberculosis after the 1870s; and after Robert Koch published his discovery of the bacillus of the disease in 1884, towns and cities took steps to control the sale of food and milk which might carry the infection. But although there was growing awareness of what caused tuberculosis there were no facilities for its treatment in Scotland, apart from ordinary infirmaries. Quarrier wanted to change this.

He first broached the subject of helping children with the disease as early as 1888 in his *Narrative of Facts*;

> For some years past, we have greatly felt the need of a house where older boys suffering from consumption and other diseases could be cared for. To build a Home for this purpose, £2,000 would be required, and we look to the Lord to incline one or more of His stewards to do this piece of service for Him. Bethesda, our Home for invalid girls and little boys, has been fully occupied throughout the whole of the year, and, as four of our older lads have died in the Infirmary – where we had to send them, not having a separate place to nurse them in – and many consumptive and delicate ones have had to be refused admission to the Homes, we are very desirous to have a house where we would be privileged to care for such.

At this stage Quarrier envisaged a new home especially for consumptive children where they could be isolated and treated away from the healthy ones. But by 1893, when he returned to the subject, he had a much bigger project in mind. In the *Narrative of Facts* for that year he proposed to build two hospitals on land adjoining the Orphan Homes, one for females and one for males, where anyone from the age of four to thirty who was orphaned or destitute could be treated. The hospitals were to be for old and young, men and women, for the whole of Scotland – and they would be free.

Quarrier had done a good deal of research and had travelled to England to visit the Royal National Hospital for Consumption at Ventnor, on the Isle of Wight, and the Hospital for Consumption in London. The Brompton Hospital, opened in 1846, was built on the block and ward system of an ordinary infirmary and could accommodate nearly 350 patients, but Quarrier preferred the set-up at Ventnor; there the patients lived in separate rooms in spacious airy houses which reduced the risk of infection. This was what he had in mind for his own hospitals – there would be two separate blocks with accommodation for twenty patients, and each patient would have his or her own room or, at the most, share with one other person. There was no such place in Scotland. As the 1893 *Narrative of Facts* said, this would be the country's first free consumptive hospital and Quarrier believed it would be a success.

Within weeks of announcing his plans for the hospitals, Quarrier had received the promise of £7,500 to build the first one, and other donations followed quickly. He had had his eye on the farm of Carsemeadow which adjoined the Orphan Homes, and when it came on the market he stepped in and bought 86½ acres for £6,722. Building could now begin and on 5 September 1894 the foundation stone of the first hospital was laid. It was a bold and responsible undertaking and Quarrier had surrounded himself with the leading medical men of his day as an advisory board, among them Dr William Gairdner and Dr James Russell, both former Medical Officers of Health for Glasgow.

After the excitement and expectation of the laying of the foundation stone, hopes of admitting the first patient within just two years were high, but things did not go according to plan. Work began on the first hospital and the executive buildings, where the steam boilers, Turkish

The laying of the memorial stone of the Consumption Hospital by Sir William Arrol, 5 September 1894

baths and inhalation rooms were to be housed, and both were officially opened on 3 September 1896; but it was to be another two years before the first patient was admitted. Problems with drainage and the new sewerage system caused many headaches for Quarrier, and he must have wondered if his hospital would ever be ready.

But at last it was. On 27 May 1898 the first woman patient was admitted to Scotland's first hospital for consumptives. This 'Riviera in Renfrewshire', as it had been dubbed at the official opening, was ready to receive women from all over the country and try to effect a cure for their suffering. But it became evident after only nine months that the system of warm-air ventilation was not having the desired results – it seemed that the Riviera regime of steam baths, inhalation sessions and heated bedrooms did not improve the health of the patients significantly. So, after a year, and just a few months before a second hospital for women was opened, Quarrier announced a change of treatment and a change of name. Instead of pumping warm air into all the rooms to keep them at a constant high temperature, he adopted the Continental open-air system which meant plenty of fresh air and outdoor exercise in all weathers for the patients. The ventilation machines were switched off, all the windows were thrown wide open, day and night, and the Consumption Hospitals at Bridge of Weir became the Consumption Sanatoria.

In the *Narrative of Facts* of 1899 Quarrier gives a vivid account of this new treatment that every patient underwent, or rather, I suspect, had to endure:

The patients usually reach us with the temperature varying from 100 to 103, and on arrival they are sent to bed until the temperature gets normal, the windows and doors of bedrooms being kept open night and day. During their stay in bed they must eat large quantities of food and drink quantities of sweet milk. After the temperature has reached its normal state, as shown on the chart marked daily, the patient is allowed to rise and go out, the doctor regulating the length of walking exercise to be taken. The patients are not allowed to walk out in large numbers, but alone or with one companion, so as to avoid excitement in talking. The rising hour is seven o'clock, and after bathing, dressing, etc., breakfast is served at eight o'clock, consisting of ham and eggs, fish or other meats, with a good supply of bread and plenty of butter, a pint of warm milk, and finishing with a cup of tea, if desired. After breakfast and examination by the doctor, they walk out in all weathers, returning to the house at twelve o'clock to rest for an hour before lunch at one o'clock. This meal consists of roast beef, mutton, tongue or other meat, amounting to half a pound after being cooked, to each patient, with potatoes and other vegetables and followed by a good supply of pudding. A pint of sweet milk is also taken with this meal. If patients cannot eat there is little hope of recovery, and it is necessary on their part to exercise a good deal of will power, as well as supervision on the part of the doctor and nurses, to see this part of the treatment carried through. The doctor presides at meals, and insists that, even if they have to sit for two hours or more, the quantities prescribed must be partaken of . . .

The afternoon is mostly occupied with short walks and rest in the open-air couches, or, when stormy, in the open-air shelters provided in the grounds. Rain does the patients no harm, and they are out in all weathers. A mackintosh is not allowed to be used, as it causes perspiration . . . After an hour's rest, dinner is served at seven o'clock, where, as at lunch, half a pound of meat, with potatoes and vegetables, etc., must be disposed of by each patient, followed by a good supply of pudding, and finishing up with fruit and plenty of sweet milk. After dinner there is quiet rest, and all must be in bed by nine o'clock, with windows and doors open all night.

It's a fascinating account of the earliest methods used to tackle a killer disease without any of the tuberculin injections which were developed years later. Apart from stuffing their patients with food and drink, all that the doctors at the sanatoria could do in these early days was to try to guard against infection by burning the patient's handkerchiefs every day and regularly examining their sputum under the microscope until no trace of the tuberculosis bacilli could be detected.

Until 1901 the sanatoria at Bridge of Weir remained the only place in Scotland for the special treatment of the disease. In that year the Glasgow and West of Scotland branch of the National Association for the Prevention of Consumption, formed at the turn of the century, donated £500 towards the cost of a sanatorium at Bellefield in Glasgow; and three years later they recognised the pioneering work at Bridge of Weir by granting £5,000 to the sanatoria over five years. A third sanatorium, for men, was added to Bridge of Weir in 1907, which made it the largest centre for the treatment of consumption anywhere in Scotland.

The year after the Congress on Tuberculosis which Quarrier attended in London in 1900, Queen Victoria died. When she had acceded to the throne in 1837 William Quarrier was just eight years old and starting an apprenticeship as a shoemaker; on her death she left behind a British Empire which ruled a quarter of the world's peoples and was more powerful and influential than it had ever been. Quarrier was seventy-two when Victoria died. In the thirty years since he had opened his first home for orphans in Renfrew Lane, 13,000 children had passed through his hands and more than £500,000 had been sent in from people all over the world. His Orphan Homes at Bridge of Weir had grown into a village with everything from a church to a fire station, inhabited by many hundreds of children. And he had given Scotland its first free sanatoria for consumption.

He launched his last big project in 1901, one which he had been thinking about for many years. In his 1893 *Narrative of Facts* he had described some of the terrible physical disabilities suffered by the orphans he had been dealing with for nearly thirty years;

> During the twenty-nine years of our work amongst poor children we have had under our care about 10,000 children and young people. Among these there have been many deformed, helpless and incurable ones. Some of these have been born without hands, others without a leg; some of them being worsted in the battle of life, have lost some of their members, and again others have spinal and hip-joint diseases, while some are afflicted with epilepsy, a most distressing form of disease.

It was this last class of sufferers, people with epilepsy, which Quarrier now wanted to help. Very little was known about the condition; it was called 'the falling sickness' and an ignorant and superstitious public believed it to be a form of insanity. In tackling the problem of epilepsy Quarrier was stepping into even more unexplored territory than the treatment of consumption had been. There was nowhere in Scotland where someone with epilepsy could be helped, but in England new ideas about how to treat the condition had been developing over the previous few years.

Europe saw the first examples of small communities, usually in rural areas, where people with epilepsy could live and work, away from the prejudices and pressures of life in the outside world. The practice spread to England and many such communities – or colonies, as they were named by the enthusiastic pioneers who started them – began to appear all over the country. In 1901 Quarrier visited one of the best-known, the Chalfont Colony for Epileptics, in Buckinghamshire,

COLONY OF MERCY FOR EPILEPTICS.

WE give our friends above a more finished picture of the first house in the Colony than we were able to furnish in last report. It will be seen that the place is gradually taking on a more " homelike " appearance. This house was opened more than three months ago and is proving well suited for the object for which it was designed.

Reproduced from the 1906 Narrative of Facts

opened in 1893, where 136 men and women lived in six houses, supervised by staff. The colonists lived and worked together with the staff, were taught trades and did light work each day. Quarrier also visited the Maghull Home for Epileptics, near Liverpool, which was run on similar lines.

Scotland was far behind England and the rest of the civilised world in treating epilepsy, and there were no such centres anywhere in the country. The poorhouse or asylum were the only places for men, women and children with epilepsy whose family could not look after them, or who had no family, and Quarrier estimated that there were some 4,000 sufferers all over the country. He wanted to build a Colony of Mercy for them, as he called it. His plan was to buy more land beside the Homes and build six houses, rather like the children's cottages, two for men, two for women and two for boys and girls, at a cost of about £20,000. There the colonists would live together in a home-

Last snapshot of William Quarrier, taken on the front at Millport,
11 August 1903

like atmosphere, doing light work such as gardening, getting plenty of
outdoor exercise and helping round the village. Like the sanatoria, the
colony would be national and anyone from Scotland would be eligible
for admission for a small weekly charge.

Donations began to pour in from all over the country and in 1902
Quarrier bought 213 acres of Hattrick Farm which adjoined the Homes
land. He had consulted closely with many medical men. However,
in those early days, before powerful drugs and advanced electronic
equipment for scanning the brain had been developed, the Colony of
Mercy could only offer healthful air and pleasant, open surroundings,
which Quarrier hoped might relieve some of the anxieties and stresses
of the patients. He described his approach in this way in the 1902
Narrative of Facts:

> Our aim is to provide this open door where afflicted ones may be sent with
> the assurance that all that medical skill and sanctified common sense can do
> for them will be lovingly rendered.

'Sanctified common sense' – what an apt description of the characteristic which informed all of Quarrier's work.

William Quarrier did not live to see the opening in 1906 of the first home of what was, and still is today, the only place in Scotland exclusively devoted to the treatment and care of people with epilepsy. A year after he had bought Hattrick Farm, and just two weeks short of completing thirty-nine years of work with Scotland's children, William Quarrier died, on 16 October 1903.

He had become ill at the beginning of the month with the kidney trouble which had dogged him all his life. His condition became alternately better and worse until at midnight on Tuesday, 13 October, he suffered a stroke that left him paralysed down the right side. He never properly regained consciousness and died in the early hours of the Friday morning. Thousands attended his funeral from far and wide and the flag above the City Chambers in Glasgow flew at half-mast. Friends and relatives, workers and colleagues, joined hundreds of children in the Homes Church, Mount Zion, for a simple service, and

The gravestones of the Quarrier family in Mount Zion churchyard

afterwards William Quarrier was buried in the little cemetery in the grounds of the church. The inscription on his coffin read:

Entered into rest, October 16, 1903, aged 74, William Quarrier, friend of the poor and needy, and founder of the Orphan Homes of Scotland.

Quarrier's son-in-law and right-hand-man, David J. Findlay, described him as Scotland's greatest philanthropist; the obituary in the *Glasgow Herald* said that a unique personality had been lost. Quarrier was a compelling figure, a man years before his time who, single-handed, challenged grave social problems with which the public authorities of his day could not cope. He was spurred on always by an acute sense of personal responsibility, as a Christian and as a member of the community. He had suffered great privation and hardship himself as a boy; as he grew up he saw the same need and distress all around him, and he knew that he must fight it.

He was a man of incredible energy and enthusiasm who was always seeing new work to be done, always interested in every aspect of the work in progress. There is a story that during the construction of the first cottages at Bridge of Weir he could often be seen out early in the morning, checking the walls with a spirit level. He loved to be in the thick of things and there was a strong streak of the fighter in him, that same streak which helped him survive a hard childhood and brought him success as a businessman.

Everything he did had flair and dare. He once challenged the editor of the *Glasgow Herald*, who had criticised his emigration work, to come with him into the heart of the city slums and see the kind of children he was trying to help: 'See for yourself the misery and wretchedness which it is impossible to describe,' he wrote to the editor, and 'accompany me with a band of rescued ones to Canada.' If the editor found Quarrier's claim that the majority of his children did well in new homes in Canada to be wrong, Quarrier would pay all his expenses for the trip; but if not, the *Glasgow Herald* would have to foot the bill. The editor did not take up the challenge.

Quarrier was a man who liked to get his own way and he was no diplomat when it came to getting things done. If something had to be done, he preferred to do it himself and would brook no interference once he had made up his mind that something was right. With committees of any kind he had very little patience, and although he worked with a great many dedicated helpers, he always liked to forge ahead on his own.

But with this strong and determined personality went great compassion and warmth. A Scot through and through, his outward manner, rather stiff and reserved, often belied an inward warmth. No one but his wife and family knew, for instance, that for more than twenty years after the death of Thomas Corbett, who gave the original £2,000 for the Renfrew Lane Home, Quarrier visited his grave every year and laid flowers there. Throughout all those years of building Homes and helping Scotland's children, William Quarrier never forgot the man whose kindness and generosity had made it all possible.

Chapter 8

Cottage Life

. . . The car sped on through towns and villages; within a mile or two of our destination the scenery became very pleasant, with green fields and horses and cattle grazing peacefully; the sun was shining a little, too. Maybe it wouldn't be so bad in a Home after all, I told myself at one point on the journey, but deep down inside me I was filled with a terror I had never known before in the short life already behind me. I tried to comfort my sister. There was someone else in the car carrying a very young baby, but she didn't take much notice of us, or I of her.

Isabel clung to me more than ever when she realised that we were approaching our destination.

We were now travelling on a very narrow road; the car had by now slowed down considerably. Soon it turned into a driveway. We had arrived.

Eventually two pathetically clad waifs entered the hall of the big grey house that was to be my home for seven and a half years and Isabel's for over three years.

We waited in the hall for a few minutes. It was a large square hall with four doors leading into rooms. However, my very first observation was not the amount of doors but a picture which hung above the door which faced the front entrance to the house. It was not really a picture at all; there were no lakes or trees on it, just words. The words I read were surrounded by little flowers and read thus: 'Christ Is The Head of This House, The Unseen Guest at Every Meal, The Silent Listener to Every Conversation'. Many times from that day I read these words and thought about them and wondered.

The day Jan Gordon saw the Orphan Homes of Scotland for the first time with her young sister is still vivid in her memory. Jan was just eleven years old and when she arrived that day at Bridge of Weir she had no idea why she was there, why her mother couldn't look after her and what was going to happen to her. What would life be like in this unfamiliar place?

There are thousands of men and women like Jan who spent part or all of their childhoods at Bridge of Weir, and many of them have contributed their memories and reflections to this book. What was life like for these boys and girls in the Orphan Homes during the first half of the twentieth century? Those were the decades when the Homes had settled into the rather rigid ways and methods of a huge charitable institution, at its best caring for thousands of children lovingly and positively; at its worst, guilty of inflexibility, regimentation and, sometimes, downright cruelty. What was it like to live in a cottage with thirty other children, and how did the cottage function from day to day? Jan entered the Homes in 1939, thirty-six years after the death of the founder. But she would have found cottage life little changed from the early years of the century because, by the time William Quarrier died, he had set in motion a pattern of life in the community he had created which continued in much the same way for half a century.

There were of course changes in management after Quarrier's death. The running of the Homes was taken over by his wife, Isabella, with an Advisory Council which consisted of Pastor David Findlay (Quarrier's son-in-law), Robert Bryden (the Homes architect) and Glasgow Councillor J.P. Maclay, a long-standing Trustee. A statement issued by the Trustees announced that everything would be run as before and no appeals would be made for funds, in accordance with the principles on which Quarrier had founded the Homes. Less than a year later, in June 1904, Mrs Quarrier died and was buried beside her husband in the cemetery of Mount Zion. Now the management of the Homes, with their 1,200 children and two Consumption Sanatoria, fell to two of Quarrier's daughters, Mary Quarrier and Mrs Agnes (Quarrier) Burges. Their sister Isabella, who was married to Pastor Findlay, did not join the Council of Management until 1931, when Mary died. The task ahead of the Quarrier family and the Executive Committee (as the Advisory Council was re-named in 1906) was a daunting one; thousands of men, women and children in the Homes were dependent upon them. But they shouldered their responsibility and the work continued unabated.

For the children in their cottages daily life was not much affected by the changes at the top. Numbers in the village remained fairly steady; there was an all-time peak in the First World War – on Armistice Day (11 November 1918), 1,550 children were resident – but throughout the inter-war years numbers were always around the 1,000 mark.

The cottages remained more or less as they had been built and were not extensively altered and re-decorated until the 1950s and 1960s. The open-sided sheds attached to each cottage, where traditionally chores such as cleaning shoes and cutlery had been done by the children, were not closed-in until 1949. More cottages were added over the years for babies and toddlers, but, essentially, the system of cottage life which Quarrier had inaugurated continued in much the same way until after the Second World War.

Christmas was a symbol of this continuity. Not until 1942 did the Homes end the old Scottish tradition of celebrating Christmas at New Year instead of on December 25. The children had to wait until New Year's Day to meet Santa Claus and receive their presents; instead they celebrated Christmas morning with a special breakfast of bacon and eggs (a change from the usual porridge, bread and margarine). The children were always making up songs about their life in the Homes and one which many former Boys and Girls remember was about that special Christmas Day breakfast:

There is a happy land
Down at Bridge of Weir,
Where we get ham and eggs
Once every year.
Oh, how the children yell
When they hear the breakfast bell,
'Oh, crikey, what a smell!'
Down at Bridge of Weir.

Usually the cottages were decorated with streamers and coloured paper, but there were no presents round the tree; there was not even a tree. Instead the children would get an apple, an orange and a bag of sweets or a bar of chocolate in their black woollen stocking, and would spend the day quietly in the cottage. The real festivities took place on New Year's Day. A special service was held in Mount Zion and on the great day each child received a present from one of the three huge Christmas trees – a tree for the boys, one for the girls and the other for the sick children in Bethesda and Elim Homes and the Elise Hospital. The gifts were always brand new – toys, games, books and dolls bought by the staff from a list of things the children wanted. It was always a time of great excitement when your cottage-mother asked you what you wanted for Christmas. There was, alas, no guarantee that you would get what you asked for, however – one former Boy remembers his disgust at receiving a Bible after he had asked for a pair of leather gloves.

The Homes did their children proud on such special occasions. Despite the straitened circumstances of both world wars, years when prices shot up, when sweets and sugar were rationed and soldiers got most of the chocolate that was going, the children at Bridge of Weir never missed their Christmas and New Year's treats. Donations from an ever-generous public continued to flood in throughout the particularly severe years of the First World War. Even in 1916, when the cottages were bursting at the seams with soldiers' children and food costs had soared (the Homes' butcher's bill rose from £4,000 a year to £6,000 in just two years), still the *Narrative of Facts* could report that every need had been met and the accounts balanced.

Two weeks' holiday down the Clyde was another special time for the children. In 1919 a friend gifted two houses on the Firth of Clyde near Dunoon – Torr Aluinn and Hoop House – for the exclusive use of the Homes, and each summer large parties of children travelled down for a holiday. Many of the orphaned, abandoned, desperately poor and ill-treated children who came to the Homes would never normally have had a holiday, and for them this was a thrilling time. All the girls received new summer frocks and hundreds of pairs of sandals were issued for those long days on the beach.

The parties consisted of about 250 children. On the great day the older ones marched in an enormous two-by-two crocodile to Kilmacolm Station, two and a half miles away, the younger ones going on ahead by bus. The excitement would mount as everyone packed into the train for Gourock and then – what delight to arrive at the busy quay and board the steamer! John Howatson was in the Homes in the 1930s and still remembers vividly the fun of that trip down the Clyde:

> Hunter's Quay, Kirn, Dunoon, all the hustle and bustle of quayside activity; and, after leaving Dunoon, there was the preparation of watching for the first

Torr Aluinn, near Dunoon

glimpse of Torr Aluinn, which stood on a raised mound of ground with a central tower, and from the tower someone frantically waving a tablecloth; tremendous cheers emitted from many throats, many Paisley design hankies were held up to flutter like flags. Then the Skipper blew a long blast from the ship's whistle which drowned out our cheers.

House-mothers would give out sandwiches during the trip and word always got around if Cottage Forty-one was on board. The mother of that cottage, Ma Broon as she was known, used to make her boys spiced dumpling for the voyage, and there was always plenty left to share with others.

Each child was given pocket money to buy sweets or trinkets during the holiday. Catharine Hopkins, who went to the Homes in 1906, remembered that when she used to go on holiday to another Homes cottage in Rothesay, the great favourites to buy with your holiday penny were treacle toffees, four Blackjacks (sweets), a rubber ball or a skipping rope. Then there were all the usual games on the beach – races, sandcastle competitions, throwing competitions, looking for shells and lots of inter-cottage games. And sometimes, when invention

Hoop House, near Dunoon

had been exhausted, the children sat in groups on the sand and sang songs, like the one about the infamous Buck Ruxton who murdered his wife and who, the children would whisper, owned the blue boat anchored in the bay below Torr Aluinn:

> Blood stains on the carpet,
> Blood stains on the knife,
> Oh, Doctor Buck Ruxton,
> You murdered your wife.
> Nurse Mary was watching,
> You thought she would tell,
> Oh, Doctor Buck Ruxton,
> You killed her as well.

Holidays, Christmas, Hallowe'en, Easter – these were the highspots, the red-letter occasions of every child's calendar. They earned these treats, though, because the rest of the time they worked hard. By the 1960s every cottage in the Homes employed cleaners and other full-time domestic staff for the general running of the cottage. The children helped with beds and doing the dishes, but most of the work was done for them. Things were very different in earlier years. 'We ran the place,' said William McCutcheon, who grew up in the Homes during the Second World War. Every child in the cottage, from school age upwards, participated in the cleaning, scrubbing, polishing, cooking and mending regime, which was done every day. In the early years of the century the older children were up at 5 a.m. to scrub the outside steps and pathway to the cottage; a full day's cleaning of the house, from top to bottom, had to be done before school.

The rising hour got a little later as the years passed and by the 1930s it was between 6 a.m. and 6.30 a.m. But the virtues of tidiness, cleanliness, hard work and the conscientious carrying-out of each household chore did not change. Jan Gordon, who went into the Homes in 1939, remembers in astonishing detail her first experience of this domestic efficiency. When she arrived at her allotted cottage she and her sister were taken upstairs for a bath:

> The girls ran the bath, about three inches of lukewarm water . . . We were placed in the bath together and duly scrubbed with red soap and a scrubber which seemed to be made of nails. Our hair was washed with the black Derbac soap and rinsed and washed again. Our hair was fine-tooth combed. The girls were kindly to us, and were doing their job in the conscientious manner expected of them . . . Finally we were dried and clad in white starchy nightgowns and green slippers about two sizes too big. We sat on a form until the girls had cleaned the bath and scrubbed the wooden draining board on the concrete floor with a big scrubbing brush; then, still on their knees, they washed and dried the surrounding floor. The girls then folded the canvas towels used on us, neatly, and placed them in a laundry basket. Nothing, I learned, was ever thrown; everything was folded neatly; even the smallest undergarment 'out for washing' was folded meticulously.

Each task had to be done properly or it had to be done again. Even the youngest children had to learn this. They often began by polishing the cutlery, starting with the spoons. This was in the days before tins of silver polish, so the children had to mix up whitening powder in water and then rub it on. The spoons were easiest because of the large surface area; it was when you had to clean the forks and make sure that no whitening was left in between the prongs that it became tiresome.

Boot-cleaning was another daily task. Each cottage had a huge boot rack in the hallway with dozens of pairs of shoes, black ones for summer, brown ones for Sundays and special occasions, and black lace-up boots

Girls at work in the Wash-house

for winter. In the days before Cherry Blossom, shoes were cleaned by mixing big slabs of boot black in water and meticulously rubbing it into the leather. It was quite common for a child of seven or eight to have ten pairs of boots to clean every day after school.

Boys had to do all the domestic chores which girls did, from cooking to cleaning. When a boy reached school-leaving age he usually did a year's full-time work as a kitchen boy in his cottage. After this he would probably spend a year with one of the tradesmen in the Homes learning the basics of a trade to prepare him for the day he left, at sixteen. The same applied to the girls, except that they would spend a year or so in the laundry or patch room or helping in the Elise Hospital or Baby Homes. Most of the girls leaving at sixteen went into careers as domestic servants or nurses.

From the age of about ten, boys and girls were allocated certain jobs for a few months at a time round the cottage, designed to give them all-round experience of looking after a home. The Bedroom boy or girl made all the beds, cleaned the dormitories and swept and polished the wooden floors. It was the job of the Playroom girls and boys to help dress the younger children in the morning and get them ready for school, as well as to clean and polish the playroom daily. Bathroom duty involved bathing the little ones and cleaning the bathroom thoroughly. Some cottages even had a Potato girl or boy who had to peel a mound of potatoes for the large family every day.

The fact that boys' cottages were run the same way as the girls', with boys doing the cooking, cleaning, scrubbing and mending themselves, meant that the Orphan Homes produced a generation of men who were every bit as competent around the house as women. These men could cook, sew, knit, darn and make rag rugs; they could polish wooden floors and brass bed-knobs; and it was nothing to them to have to wash, dress and look after half-a-dozen toddlers and young boys.

A typical day for the Kitchen boy would have tested the culinary skills of most women. Under his cottage-mother's supervision he was responsible for providing three meals a day for thirty or more children. His day began at 6.30 a.m. when he was up and about preparing porridge for the breakfast. He had left the oats to soak overnight and a huge pan of water simmering on the open range. If he had banked up the range properly the night before it would be at just the right temperature and easy to stoke up for cooking. While another lad set the table and another cut and prepared slices of bread and margarine, the older boys in the cottage roused the young ones. All this time the Kitchen boy was keeping a watchful eye on the massive pan of porridge, trying to keep it hot without burning it, thick but not lumpy, in time for the serving of breakfast at about 7.45 a.m. After breakfast everyone helped with the dishes and, once the kitchen was cleared and the boys had left for school, the Kitchen boy would have to start cleaning the black range and preparing the food for dinner at 12.30 p.m. This usually consisted of soup and a main course, or a main course and pudding; mince, stew, dumpling, bread puddings – these were the staple meals. Sunday dinners consisted of roast meat of some kind, but most of the preparation for that was done the night before so that as little work as possible was done on the Sabbath.

After tea at 5.30 p.m. and cottage evening worship, the Kitchen boy was free to go out and play. Football, cricket in the summer, and rounders – Bridge of Weir was a great place for sport and the children spent hours, especially in the long summer evenings, playing in the park. Other evening activities included the Girl Guides, the Boys' Brigade, the Young Lad's Christian Association and on Saturdays the occasional film show in the church.

Sundays were strictly kept. Quarrier founded the Homes on strong Christian principles and from the start it was his avowed intention not just to rescue children from the poverty and misery of the streets and feed and clothe them, but to educate them in the Christian life as well. Every cottage-mother and -father had to hold Christian beliefs and inculcate them into the children – so much so that Catharine Hopkins, who left the Homes in 1920 to go into domestic service, thought that she had landed in the house of the devil because her mistress did sewing and other small chores on a Sunday! It was drummed into the children that it was positively wicked to break the Sabbath in any way. A walk in the afternoon, in an orderly cottage group, was the only activity allowed on a Sunday.

As well as family worship every day in the cottages, there were services at 11 a.m. and 6 p.m. on a Sunday in Mount Zion. Each cottage had its allotted pew in the church, and every Sunday the rows would teem with children of all ages and sizes. There was no regular preacher to

Homelea and Paisley Home

conduct the services. Until the appointment of the then Chairman, Dr James Kelly, as Honorary Pastor in the 1950s, services were conducted each week by visiting ministers from all over Scotland.

It was said by the children that Dr Kelly always knew if a single child were missing from the church services. And it was always a tense moment when he peered thoughtfully around the crowded hall, considering which cottage to ask to recite that week's text. This was a regular task for the children. The Homes issued a calendar with a different Bible text for each week. Every cottage was expected to learn the appropriate text by heart for the following week and be able to recite it faultlessly in front of the whole church if asked. Oh, the sinking feeling if your cottage were asked to stand up and recite and you hadn't learnt it properly!

In earlier years it was the custom to choose just one child and there was an unspoken rivalry among house-mothers to have the youngest child who could give a flawless performance; the younger the child, the more credit reflected on the cottage and the house-mother. But if a text were wrongly recited, that was a black mark indeed and there would be trouble for the offender after the service. Anyone seen fidgeting, whispering or being inattentive was also liable for a telling-off or a clout back in the cottages. These services must have seemed endless to the younger children but at least they could join in the singing. Quarrier's children were always great singers. BBC Christmas broadcasts used to go out from the Homes church and many years ago two long-playing records of the children singing were produced: 'Sing with Quarrier's Children' and 'Singing for My Lord'.

Friday night was another special time of the week because that was when the cottage parents attended their own worship hour in Mount Zion. This was a time for fun and games because the children were left unattended. One former Home Girl recalls the fun her cottage used to have sliding down the stairs on a mattress and playing the harmonium which was locked away in a cupboard in the playroom – someone discovered that the lock could be picked with the key from a corned beef tin! It was always considered very daring in the girls' cottages to pass messages to boys in school, inviting them round to the cottage on a Friday evening: not only was the mixing of cottages frowned upon, except in sport, but far worse than that was the mixing of boys and girls. It was not until 1945 that Dr Kelly decided the time had come to experiment with mixed cottages for the youngest children.

Friday evenings offered opportunities for mischief and rule-breaking in an otherwise strictly controlled environment. Virtually every aspect of the children's life was regimented to some degree. Even brothers and sisters had to make an appointment to see one another outside school hours. The procedure was set down in the Homes' *Standing Orders*:

> Brothers and sisters should be afforded reasonable opportunity of being frequently together, although not living under the same roof. In the case of brothers and sisters attending school, no special provision need be made, but where they have left school or are not yet old enough to attend school, boys should be given the opportunity on Saturday afternoons between two and four o'clock to visit their sisters. If they wish to do so boys should be permitted to visit their sisters on two Saturdays in the month. The limit of the visit should be one hour. Boys should be instructed to apply at the front door to the mother of the Home where the sisters reside. House-mothers of girls' Homes will allow brothers to visit with their sisters in the Dining Room but not in the Playshed.

Of course the reasoning behind such rules was that, with more than 1,000 children to look after, you could not afford to let everybody rush off and see their siblings whenever they felt like it, or it would end in chaos. This was not an era which embraced the idea of children's individual rights and freedoms, and the Homes were of their time; this was a huge institution where the smooth running of things depended on rules and regulations. But none of that was any comfort if it was *your* sister you wanted to see, *your* sister that you missed each day. Being separated from siblings is a pain which has stayed with many former Boys and Girls to this day. James McCallum well remembers the chilling formality of his visits to his sister and how awkward and tongue-tied the unnaturalness of the situation made them both:

> I had a younger sister in the Orphans Home and in order to speak to her I had to make a formal appointment, and a day and hour would be named. I would walk up to her cottage and stand outside the fence around their play area. My sister would come out and stand inside the fence, and because of the formality of the occasion I had no words except, 'How are you, Georgina? Are you okay?' If they had allowed us to go for a walk together we would have had plenty to say to each other, but walking with a girl, even your sister, was strictly forbidden.

Lessons over for the day at the Homes' School

Being separated from your brother or sister was bad enough, but in the first half of the twentieth century it sometimes happened that children who were too young to remember them were not told that they did, in fact, have brothers and sisters who were actually living in the Homes.

Some men and women only discovered years after they left the Homes that they'd had a brother or sister there all the time and had never been informed. Sometimes, if they were lucky, they might be able to track each other down in the outside world, but not always. Whether this was bureaucratic carelessness, institutional indifference or deliberate policy on the part of the Homes of that era, it was unacceptable and the present Quarriers organisation has readily acknowledged that. Every former Boy or Girl has the right to see their own records, and Quarriers is only too glad to help anyone who wants to find out more about their family background and possible sibling separation.

Back in the first half of the twentieth century, openness and attention to individual rights were not the Homes' way. This was an era of rigidly enforced rules and uniform practices. Everything was done at a set time and in a set way. When walking to church on a Sunday morning, many cottage-mothers insisted that the children marched in a crocodile, two abreast, those on the right carrying their Bibles in their right hand and those on the left flank carrying them in their left. In many cottages it was the practice for the children to march upstairs to bed at night, or march out of the house to school, in a long single line, the youngest first and the oldest bringing up the rear.

Mealtimes were equally strict. No talking at the table was the rule in past years. Clare Macnair lived in the Homes from 1929 to 1943, and in her cottage not only did the girls have to file in to each meal in order of age, but had to show their clean white handkerchiefs to the mother who stood at the door. There would certainly be trouble if you lost that precious cotton square; but if you pulled through a corner of your white apron so that it stuck up from your fist like a hankie, it was sometimes possible to escape retribution.

Generally, however, most former Girls and Boys who have shared their experiences of that era have said that they took the rules and regulations in their stride. For some, in the Homes since their earliest years, it was all they had known and it was a natural, accepted way of life. There was a great camaraderie and friendship among the children

Dinner-time in Lincoln and Garfield Cottage

in every cottage, a warmth and family feeling which was strong; the Homes were never a proper home but, as one former Girl remarked, 'The children made their own happiness', and, for many, life at Bridge of Weir was far better than what they would normally have had. 'I never went hungry, I was never ragged,' recalls David Wilson. 'I never knew want, I never wanted for anything. In short, it was a better life and upbringing than I could ever have had with my mother.'

But more than anything, the quality of life in the Homes depended on the cottage parents, particularly the cottage-mother. There were far too many children in each cottage to allow much closeness and affection between mother and child, but there could be trust and kindliness. Most of the men and women who looked after the children were ordinary, kindly people; they were not trained for the great responsibility and it can have been no easy task for a cottage-mother seventy years ago, who might have as many as thirty-five boys of all ages to look after all day; and in a place the size of the Homes it was inevitable that some cottage parents made a better job of it than others. Some former Girls and Boys remember their cottage parents with great affection; for them they were truly surrogate parents. Others were not so lucky and never enjoyed a close relationship. Martha Nixon went into the Homes in 1935 at the age of eight. Although her sister was in the same cottage, she desperately missed her real mother and could get no comfort from the cottage-mother. 'I never could cuddle or kiss her,' she said. 'She was terribly strict'.

And there were others who have the awful and ineradicable memory of years spent with cottage parents who were not fit to look after children. Discipline for all children in the Homes was, by today's standards, strict; but there were a few men and women who most certainly punished the children in their care excessively, and in some cases treated them with unbelievable cruelty.

The memories of Jan Gordon, who was in the Homes from 1939 to 1946, read like something out of *Oliver Twist*. She has written about her life at Bridge of Weir in an unpublished personal narrative which she calls *Along Life's Narrow Way*. The most harrowing descriptions in this vivid account are of the way in which her younger sister was treated. Her sister's crime was that she was not prepared to eat the lumps in her porridge:

> My sister was the worst offender. Miss Morrison[*] . . . would drag her out of the seat by her hair, and make her stand beside the unlit fireplace facing the serving table; she would slap her about then push the plate into her hands. Sometimes she stuck her face into it, eventually castor oil was poured over it and she would be force-fed with the help of an older girl, Miss Morrison ramming it down her throat . . If she was not at school she would be made to stand on her head in a corner of the hall.

Jan's sister was only five at the time. Such treatment would be almost impossible to believe if another girl who was in the same cottage for part of the time, from 1931 to 1941, had not duplicated some of the incidents recounted by Jan. Margaret Gatt describes the appalling treatment bed-wetters received in this cottage.

> In the morning you were punished by having castor oil poured over your porridge or tablespoons of Epsom Salts forced down your throat or sprinkled over your porridge; you willed yourself to keep it down . . . On the other

[*] This is not the real name of that cottage-mother

hand you could be dragged up the stairs by the hair of your head, or by your feet, with your head bumping all the way up.

Bed-wetting seems to have been a common problem in the Homes. The Standing Orders refer to 'the objectionable habits of children who are bed-wetters' and instruct house-mothers, in every case, to report it 'to the Medical Officer and his instruction as to treatment carried out as far as possible. No treatment should be given apart from such direction'. Despite these instructions, one 'treatment' administered by callous house-mothers in some cottages was for the child to be thrown into a bath of cold water. The earliest memory of Catharine Hopkins, who went to the Homes in 1906 at the age of three, was of being dragged downstairs by the hair and punished in this way because she had wet her bed.

The worst thing was that there was little help for it if a child happened to be in a 'bad' cottage. For children under the thumb of a cruel house-mother or -father, complaining was out of the question; they would probably be punished for that, too. They were powerless. Besides, the children had virtually no contact with the higher authorities in the Homes, and each cottage could function quite independently inside its four walls. A child could be cruelly mistreated and few outside the cottage would know about it.

There is no doubt that there were some men and women working as house-parents in the Homes in that era who should never have been allowed to have charge of children. They were untrained, there were no police or security checks in those days, and they had more or less a free hand within the walls of the cottage and the Homes. There was certainly a different attitude to physical punishment in those days, but those who experienced physical abuse as children don't complain about being spanked or having to endure strict discipline. What they are describing, by any standards, is cruelty and excessive physical punishment. Whether this was tolerated, or not known about, by the managers of the day is difficult to say, but a 'Spare the rod, and spoil the child' mentality and culture could bring out the worst in some staff. 'She was a good Christian woman' was said of one house-mother from that era; yet this was a 'Christian' who locked children in cupboards all night, or put them under the floorboards. Occasionally, however, cases of extreme punishment did find their way to the ears of those in charge. This is a letter written in 1937 by the then chairman, Dr James Kelly:[*]

> To the Fathers in Charge of the boys' cottages
>
> I am sorry to have to write this letter but I do so at the request of the Executive Committee.
>
> Several cases of extreme corporal punishment meted out to lads have been brought to our notice within recent date. One of these complaints has come from the Royal Scottish Society for the Prevention of Cruelty to Children, another from a donor and another from a Visitor. The receipt of such reports has vexed me very much. I do not wish to enter into the reason which may, or may not, have been the cause for the punishments, but I wish to express my own personal conviction with regard to excessive corporal punishment. Severe thrashing not only makes nervous wrecks of some boys, but hardens others, and produces defiance rather than penitence. It blunts the sensibility at a time when it is most desirable that the boy should be awakened by an intelligent understanding of his wrong-doing and an attempt made to secure a response to efforts for his welfare. A boy who has been severely thrashed loses respect for the person who did the thrashing. 'Thrashing' is wrong and represents a denial of that which is good in every boy, even the most troublesome.
>
> I trust that all who receive this letter will accept it in the spirit in which it has been written and help to remove from the life of the Village this loathsome and, I believe, unnecessary form of punishment.
>
> May I conclude by saying I am not unmindful of the difficulty of running either the cottage or the Village life of our Community and I do appreciate the services rendered by all our fellow workers.

It would be wrong to end an account of cottage life in the Homes in the first half of the twentieth century with stories of cruelty and beatings, because they do not represent the true spirit and quality of life for the great majority of children. Some, it is true, look back on their life in the Homes with great pain and bitterness, and with good reason. They have been scarred by their experiences; their trust in the Christian organisation which was responsible for their care and well-being was cruelly betrayed; the men and women who were charged with protecting and nurturing them, hurt and abused them instead. But they are outnumbered by those who remember Bridge of Weir

---

[*] I have not found any documentary evidence of whether any action was taken against house-parents guilty of cruelty.

with a positive sense of the chance for life which it gave them. At a time when many orphans went to the poorhouse, and abandoned children did not have the protection of a modern network of social care, the Homes at Bridge of Weir offered help and shelter. They clothed, fed, educated and brought up thousands and thousands of children who might otherwise have suffered great hardship.

Nellie Hood, who lived in the Homes from 1918 to 1927, was in no doubt of what she gained there:

> The Homes made me what I am today and I'm proud of what I am.

Chapter 9

Changes

It was May 1941. On the sixth and seventh of that month the town of Greenock, William Quarrier's birthplace, was bombed by the Germans. And just a few miles to the south, across the hills, the children in the Orphan Homes of Scotland watched the glow in the night sky cast by the burning buildings, the whisky distillery and the sugar refineries.

The war years were exciting years for the children: hearing the bombers droning overhead on their way to targets all along the Lower Clyde; huddling together in the box room under the stairs until the

The Land Army (from the Narrative of Facts, *1942)*

Ploughing for Victory (from the Narrative of Facts, *1941)*

'All Clear', sipping cups of cocoa and nibbling bread and margarine; walking to school in the morning carrying your gas mask on your arm. Thrilling times for the children, perhaps, but air-raids and black-outs were a headache for the Superintendent and his staff. Blacking-out upwards of ninety buildings all over the village was a mammoth task and it was just as well that the policeman at Kilmacolm lived in a house overlooking the Homes – he could spot any chink of light from his vantage point and telephone the Superintendent to put it right.

The war did not disrupt the even flow of life very much at the Homes, but one or two sacrifices had to be made. The annual Hallowe'en procession with turnip lanterns had to be stopped because of the black-out, and the holiday homes at Dunoon – Torr Aluinn and Hoop House – were taken over by the Navy. And, worst of all for the children, they had to watch while, one by one, the iron swings in the backyard of every cottage were dismantled and taken away to be melted down for the war effort.

But generally life continued in much the same way as usual. Rationing was not a problem and the Homes never went short of basic supplies

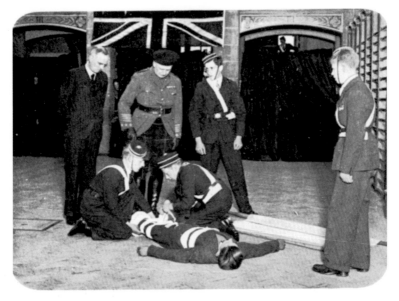

The air-raid casualty at the Boys' Brigade inspection
(from the Narrative of Facts, *1940)*

since the farm at Hattrick was well supplied with dairy cows and hens, and they had their own vegetable plots and greenhouses.

The war in Europe ended on 7 May 1945 – VE-Day. Eleven days later the news spread round the Orphan Homes village that Isabella Findlay, the eldest and last surviving daughter of the founder, had died. They were all gone now: William Quarrier and his wife, their youngest daughter Mary (who had died in 1931), and her sister Agnes, who had died three years later. Pastor David Findlay, the husband of Isabella and, since Quarrier's death, an active force in the life of the Homes, had died in 1938. The only surviving figure from the early days was Lord Maclay who, as Glasgow Councillor John P. Maclay, had become one of the Advisory Council of the Homes on Quarrier's death. In 1926, when the Homes became a non profit-making limited company under the title of the Orphan Homes of Scotland, Lord Maclay acted as Chairman of the Council of Management. Now that post was held by Dr James Kelly, but Lord Maclay was still closely associated with the Homes as Honorary President.

The end of the war marked sixty-seven years since the opening of the Homes at Bridge of Weir. There were 1,227 children in the forty-three cottages, referred from all over Scotland by officers of the RSSPCC, by local authorities and directly by relatives. More than 200 of these children were babies and toddlers living in three cottages which had been built for them over the previous fifteen years – Campbell-Snowdon, Laing-Shrewsbury and Campbell-Maltman Homes. The war had put a strain on the accommodation resources of the Homes: hundreds of children had lost a father temporarily or permanently; some had been made homeless by the bombing; others were admitted because their mother, with perhaps four or five other children to look after at home, simply could not cope. It all added up to lots of extra children, and some cottages were bursting at the seams.

Local authorities, too, faced the problem of children affected by the war. Many boys and girls were evacuated from the big cities to safer areas and the local authorities had the responsibility of boarding them out. It was during this period of upheaval that concerns began to be expressed about the plight of homeless children in public care. In England the case of Denis O'Neill brought to light the need for administrative reform in how local authorities managed the care of children. Denis and his two younger brothers and a sister had been taken from their home in 1939 by officers of the NSPCC and handed over to the local authority, which boarded them out. In 1944 Denis was moved from one foster home and sent to another, a farm in Shropshire. Some months later, as a result of continual ill-treatment and neglect on that farm (of which the authorities were never aware because no one checked up on him), Denis died. An independent inquiry under Sir Walter Monkton KC investigated the whole incident and reported that there had been grave administrative muddles, a lack of effective supervision by the local authority social workers and, for that matter, a great lack of properly trained and skilled social workers.

Public attention had been drawn to the same question of children in care just a few months earlier by a letter which appeared in *The Times* on 15 July 1944. It was headed 'Whose Children? Wards of State or Charity?', and was written by Lady Marjory Allen of Hurtwood, the wife of the First Baron Allen of Hurtwood, and Chairman of the Nursery Schools Association of Great Britain. Her letter was an eloquent expression of a new crusading spirit for reform which was emerging from the upheaval of war:

Sir,

Thoughtful consideration is being given to many fundamental problems, but in reconstruction plans one section of the community has, so far, been entirely forgotten.

I write of those children who, because of their family misfortune, find themselves under the guardianship of a government department or one of the many charitable organisations. The public are, for the most part, unaware that many thousands of these children are being brought up under repressive conditions that are generations out of date and are unworthy of our traditional care for children. Many who are orphaned, destitute or neglected still live under the chilly stigma of 'charity'; too often they form groups isolated from the main stream of life and education, and few of them know the comfort and security of individual affection. A letter does not allow space for detailed evidence.

In many 'Homes', both charitable and public, the willing staff are, for the most part, overworked, underpaid and untrained; indeed, there is no recognised system of training. Inspection for which the Ministry of Health, the Home Office, or the Board of Education may be nominally responsible is totally inadequate, and few standards are established or expected. Because no one government department is fully responsible, the problem is the more difficult to tackle.

A public inquiry, with full government support, is urgently needed to explore this largely uncivilised territory. Its mandate should be to ascertain whether the public and charitable organisations are, in fact, enabling these children to lead full and happy lives, and to make recommendations how the community can compensate them for the family life they have lost. In particular the inquiry should investigate what arrangements can be made (by regional reception centres or in other ways) for the careful consideration of the individual children before they are finally placed with foster-parents or otherwise provided for; how the use of large residential homes can be avoided; how staff can be appropriately trained and ensured adequate salaries and suitable conditions of work, and how central administrative responsibility can best be secured so that standards can be set and can be maintained by adequate inspection.

The social upheaval caused by the war has not only increased this army of unhappy children, but presents the opportunity for transforming their conditions. The Education Bill and the White Paper on the Health Services have alike ignored the problem and the opportunity.

Yours sincerely,
MARJORY ALLEN OF HURTWOOD
Hurtwood House, Albury, Guildford   15 July 1944

Less than a year after this challenging letter was written, and following on the Monkton Inquiry, two committees, one for Scotland and the other for England and Wales, were charged by the government of the day to:

> enquire into existing methods of providing for children who, from loss of parents or from any other cause whatever, are deprived of a normal life with their own parents or relatives; and to consider what further measures should be taken to ensure that these children are brought up under conditions best calculated to compensate them for the lack of parental care.

The two committees, the Scottish one chaired by Mr J.L. Clyde KC, and the English one by Miss Myra Curtis, spent seventeen months investigating all aspects of the current care of children, both statutory and voluntary, and the recommendations they made were very similar.

The Clyde report is a fascinating document, a compelling piece of social history which asks questions about the responsibility of the individual and society towards its children with the same earnestness Quarrier had shown in the previous century. The report placed the emphasis, as Quarrier had, on recreating the family:

> The lesson which above all else the war years have taught us is the value of home. It is upon the family that our position as a nation is built, and it is to the family that in trouble and disaster each child naturally turns. It is the growing awareness of the importance of the family which has largely brought into prominence the problem of the homeless child. How then is the family to be re-created for the child who is rendered homeless?

There were, at that time, three ways of dealing with homeless children in Scotland: they could be boarded out with foster parents (a practice with a long tradition in Scotland); they could be sent to voluntary homes, like the Orphan Homes; or they could go into Homes provided by the local authorities (though these were far outnumbered by voluntary homes). Of these three solutions the Clyde committee (and the Curtis committee in England and Wales) strongly favoured boarding-out or fostering as the best and most natural way to provide a good stable home for a child deprived of his or her real family. They were very much opposed to the 'outworn solution' of large institutions, the traditional orphanage of many hundreds of children in huge impersonal buildings. The committee was more impressed by the cottage home system, but stressed that if the numbers were not drastically reduced to no more than fifteen children per cottage (at this time each cottage in the Orphan Homes housed more than twenty) the children could suffer just as much as in any large institution.

But the committee did not approve of fostering without reservation. As the Denis O'Neill tragedy had shown in England, fostering could go drastically wrong and the whole system needed to be improved and reformed. There should be much more careful selection of foster parents, children should not be abandoned to the back of beyond in some remote Scottish croft (this was very common at the time), and supervision and visiting of the children should be tightened up. Even so, the report still saw the need for local authority and voluntary homes to provide for children not suitable for fostering, or who were coming into care for a short time only.

But the biggest stumbling block to achieving an effective, new, professional service for homeless children was the cumbersome and confusing administrative machinery which had been evolving for the past half century. Statutory responsibility for the care of homeless children rested with not one but three entirely different and separate bodies – public assistance authorities, education authorities and the Department of Health. And in each case the children formed only a part of their areas of responsibility. 'All this differentiation must go', declared the Clyde report. It wanted to see a specially created body whose sole responsibility was the welfare of children and which would take over all the disparate functions of the existing agencies.

The 1948 Children Act made this proposed new committee a reality. Every local authority in the country was to set up a children's committee, headed by a children's officer, a trained man or woman appointed by the local authority and approved by the Secretary of State, who would oversee and organise a team of social workers to deal with the children in the committee's local area. The Home Office was to be the sole responsible body at government level and would be advised by two advisory councils in childcare, one for Scotland and one for England and Wales.

This enthusiastic and reforming Act was called 'The Children's Charter'. At last homeless and destitute children had been made a special case. Local authorities now had a duty to receive *every* homeless, abandoned or parentless child, not just those committed to them by the courts under the Children and Young Person's Act of 1937. Very importantly, they were also required to restore a child to its parents or guardians (if it had any) as soon as possible; the idea now was to get children out of institutional care and back to normal family life in the community – an idea which would become the guiding principle behind all future developments in the care of children.

Training was also a priority in the Act. The Curtis committee in England and Wales had been so appalled by the lack of trained staff, especially in residential homes, that it brought out an interim report pleading the need for a central training council in childcare, which would initiate courses in childcare at universities and colleges. The Children Act duly made provision for government grants to finance such courses.

A new childcare service had been created, the trained childcare worker was born, old ideas were passing and new ones emerging. And where did the Orphan Homes of Scotland stand in the midst of all this? They were directly affected by the Act under a clause which required every voluntary home to be registered and regularly inspected by local authority and government officials. Indirectly the Homes were to be affected very much more because the Act shifted the direction of childcare away from residential homes to fostering, and charged state and local authorities to address themselves seriously to the task which charities and voluntary organisations had been carrying out for years. With fostering as the favoured form of care, and the onus on local authorities to try to return children to their real families, it was clear that the numbers coming into residential homes would eventually be affected. This was evident in the years after the Act came into effect: the number of children in the Orphan Homes after 1918 had remained fairly stable, at about the 1,100 or 1,200 mark, rising sharply during the Second World War, but after the 1948 Act they decreased slowly and steadily, while the numbers of children fostered and in local authority homes increased.

But the Orphan Homes and the dozens of other voluntary homes still had an indispensable role to play in the care of homeless children, as the Clyde committee concluded and the 1948 Act agreed. Accordingly, the Orphan Homes set about retrimming their sails for the task ahead. They set up their own training programmes for their staff and appointed a consultant psychiatrist to help with the emotional and psychological problems which it was now recognised many children in care experienced; they embarked on a modernisation programme for the cottages and began to reduce the numbers in each. And life inside the cottages began to change for the better; the atmosphere became less authoritarian and the children were allowed a little freedom. David Wilson, who was in the Homes from 1946 to 1956, remembers a gradual change in the 1950s:

> Things did relax somewhat, with various excursions into the outside world, like visits to Port Glasgow Baths, the Baptist Chapel in Johnstone, visits to the Kelvin Hall Circus and Calderpark Zoo. There was also a visit to Edinburgh Castle and once I went to Hampden Park.

Television came into the cottages during the 1950s, and David remembers the thrill of watching TV for the first time, on the day of the coronation of Queen Elizabeth on 2 June 1953:

The coronation parade

We sat glued to the set from dawn and never moved till transmission ended, drinking milk shakes and lots of goodies. We also received a Bible and a tin of toffees – a real special day.

Milk shakes and a Bible? Changed times, indeed.

The year 1948 brought other changes to the Orphan Homes, this time as a result of the National Health Service Act. On 5 July 1948 the Consumption Sanatoria became the responsibility of the Western Regional Hospitals Board under the 1946 Act, which brought hospitals under the administration of the government through regional boards. The three sanatoria at Bridge of Weir had treated more than 11,000 patients in the fifty years since the first unit was opened – fifty years which had seen the fight against tuberculosis won through increasingly sophisticated methods of treatment and constant research. The sanatoria started by William Quarrier had led the way in Scotland and given vital care to thousands who would otherwise have died. Some years ago the site was bought from the NHS by the company Melville Dundas and converted into a housing complex.

Before the 1950s were over, it was all-change once again at the Orphan Homes. Dr James Kelly, Chairman of the Council of Management since 1937, had felt for some time that a new post should be created in management, a full-time position for a man who would devote all his energies to running the organisation in changing times. So, in 1956, Dr Kelly was replaced as Chairman by Mr William Marr (who had recently joined the Council) and the new post of General Director was created and filled by Dr Romanes Davidson, who had been the Medical Superintendent of the Homes and Colony of Mercy since 1946. The General Director would have complete control and responsibility for the whole organisation and would be subject only to the Council. It was a post which offered great scope for imaginative, bold leadership for the future.

And to the outside world, too, the Orphan Homes presented a changed look. The Homes had been started originally to give a home to Scotland's orphans – thousands and thousands of them; and at the turn of the century orphans still formed 85 per cent of the children in the cottages. But this had been changing for many years and by the 1930s the figure was considerably lower; the eradication of most of the dreadful killer diseases, such as smallpox and typhus, had greatly increased life expectancy and children did not suffer the loss of both parents at one fell swoop as in the dark days of Victorian Scotland. It was not orphans now who formed the bulk of children in the Homes; instead there were children abandoned or deserted by their parents; the babies of unmarried mothers; children whose parents could not look after them because of illness or impossible conditions at home. In 1958, therefore, the Council of Management decided that the Homes needed a new name to reflect a new age and to honour the man who had started it all. And so the Orphan Homes of Scotland became Quarrier's Homes.

It had been an eventful decade. Now, with a new name, a new man at the top and facing the challenge of adapting to new methods of childcare in changed times, Quarrier's Homes was set on a new course for the future.

Chapter 10

After the Orphans

> He needs to like children. He must have sympathy with, rather than pity for,
> their problems and those of their parents. He must understand their views of
> the world around them. If he is to help them to come to terms with society,
> he must not only know a good deal about that society and its standards and
> values; he must himself have come to terms with it and participate in it.

That is how a 1963 report on *The Staffing of Local Authority Children's
Departments* described the qualities and abilities which every childcare
worker should possess. Caring for children had become a professional
business; the youthful, eager service which the 1948 Children Act had
created thought about itself continually and kept a faithful note of all
its doings, its new ideas and trial methods, and presented them to the
world in copious reports, studies, memoranda and official documents
throughout the 1950s and 1960s. A memorandum by the Home
Office on *The Conduct of Children's Homes* in 1952 gave instructions
on everything from the kind of staff who should be employed to the
decoration and furnishing of the children's dormitories. The Scottish
Advisory Council on Childcare (established by the 1948 Act) brought
out numerous reports on children's homes and how they could be
improved, on how children deprived of their normal home could best
be cared for, on how important it was to understand the needs of
children in care and give them security and affection.

Another regular contributor to Her Majesty's Stationery Office
bookshelves was a series of reports on *Childcare* in the 1960s, which

kept up to date with all the latest developments in the field and produced statistics on the number of children in Homes and those with foster parents. They also kept note of the reasons for children coming into care, the numbers of childcare workers and the training they were receiving.

The training of staff was a common theme of this rapidly growing body of literature. The personal qualities of the children's officer and fellow workers – an ability to communicate, a sympathetic but professional approach – were highly rated; these were skills which could not be taught, but other skills such as a knowledge of the other branches of social work which might bear upon the welfare of children, familiarity with the law relating to children, administrative skills – all these were vital matters for the childcare worker to learn. The problem was the lack of courses available in Scotland. There was a huge need for trained men and women in the children's departments but, according to *The Staffing of Local Authority Children's Departments*, not enough facilities for their training. The Scottish Education Department ran refresher courses for field staff (those who helped children in their homes and did not work in residential Homes) and for residential staff, and Langside College in Glasgow provided a course for house-parents. Edinburgh University became the first university in Scotland to offer a certificate in childcare.

Soon, however, these courses were buttressed by a multitude of others. A training committee of the Scottish Advisory Council on Childcare was set up to advise the Secretary of State on new courses, and by 1966 the situation had improved considerably. In addition to the university course at Edinburgh there was one at St Andrews and a two-year course in childcare at Moray House College of Education in Edinburgh; plans were also afoot for a one-year course for childcare officers with experience (but no qualifications) at Jordanhill College of Education in Glasgow. On top of that there was a host of short, non-certificate refresher courses for what seemed to be every subject under the sun, if the list in the 1966 report on childcare is anything to go by:

> a general course for residential staff; a course for childcare officers; a course for the staff of remand, reception and short-stay homes; a course for recent entrants to childcare field posts; a course for the heads of residential establishments

receiving students for practical placements from residential courses; a course for staff who had recently started residential work with children; a course for childcare officers, probation officers and other social workers working in isolation in rural areas; a course for the staff of homes and nurseries caring for young children; a course for staff concerned with adolescents in residential care; a course for childcare officers and probation officers receiving students for casework placements; and a course for children's officers.

A great deal of the energies of Scotland's children's departments was devoted to fostering, and there was an urgent need for childcare officers to deal with the organisation, placement and visiting of the huge army of children boarded out all over the country. The 1948 Act had given the official seal of approval to fostering as the most desirable alternative for the child and, by 1965, of the 10,457 boys and girls in the care of local authorities in Scotland, 60 per cent were boarded out with foster parents, while 1,749 were in local authority homes and 1,646 in voluntary homes.

But although it was often the most homely and natural form of care for the child, fostering was still, like residential care, only a way of helping after the event, after the situation in the real home had broken down. What the children's departments wanted most of all was to prevent the child from having to come into public care at all; they wanted to keep children with parents wherever possible. So preventative work, as it was called, became another clarion call of the childcare service in the 1960s. But what could childcare officers do in the child's real home? The 1963 Children's and Young Person's Act made it a duty of the local authorities to give any advice, guidance or assistance to families which might help to prevent problems; for example, children often came into care because their parents had been evicted for non-payment of rent, and childcare officers could offer help and advice with budgeting to avoid this. The Act also empowered them to give actual financial aid if that were necessary.

This kind of preventative work continued to grow in the 1960s; and from there it was only a short step to the thinking behind the 1968 Social Work (Scotland) Act, which abolished the children's departments and created in their place new social work departments, administering all kinds of social services, including childcare. The idea was to set up a wide-ranging *family* service which would be able to tackle the range of problems which very often lay behind the final event of family break-up and a child coming into care.

Against this rapidly moving background of childcare the numbers of children in Quarrier's Homes remained very much lower than in the years before the 1950s, but at a fairly steady level. The number stayed around the 500 mark throughout the 1960s and into the early 1970s. Of the forty-three cottages, about thirty were used for the children (the others had been converted into staff houses and used for other purposes, like extra accommodation for the Epilepsy Centre), with between fourteen and twenty children in each. Things were very different in the cottages now. The days of scrubbing the bath with Bathbrick and cooking for thirty were long gone. There were still chores to be done, beds to be made each morning, shoes cleaned and washing-up after meals. At the weekend, too, there was some cleaning and dusting to be done in the cottage, but cleaners came in during the week and did most of the housework. Mealtimes were informal affairs now, eaten in the kitchen, at three or four separate tables. There was always plenty going on in the evenings and the long summer evenings often rang with the voices of hundreds of children playing in the park down by the school. On the annual sports day, at fancy-dress parades and at Hallowe'en, the village thronged and milled with children of all ages and sizes. In the evenings they went to youth clubs, sports clubs and the uniformed organisations, and during the week they swam, played hockey and football matches against schools from outside, and went to concerts and exhibitions.

Although the number of children living in the Village was much smaller than in previous years, the turnover was higher. Children were coming into and going from Quarrier's Homes faster than ever before. They were there for shorter periods; in earlier times, when a child came into the Homes it was usually for many years, until school-leaving age, but now many children whose domestic situation for some reason was not suitable were staying for perhaps just a few months or a year, until things at the family home had improved.

Another change from earlier years was the extent of local authority responsibility for the children. By this time most of the children were referred by local authorities and only rarely directly by relatives and friends. The local authorities were also funding each child they sent, so

An aerial view of the Village taken in 1963 (reproduced by courtesy of Airviews Ltd (M/cr) Ltd, Manchester Airport)

that, slowly but surely, the balance of the Homes income shifted away from donations and legacies from the public towards maintenance grants from the various local authorities. In 1960 local authority grants totalled £40,755 and donations and legacies £181,202; by 1970 the figures were £171,161 and £216,912 respectively; by the late 1970s about 75 per cent of the Homes' income was from local authority grants for the children in their care.

These were fat years for Quarrier's Homes; donations and legacies from an ever-generous and solicitous public, supplemented by grants, kept the balance sheets very healthy, and enabled the Homes management to embark on a programme of renovation, repair and building around the Village. It certainly needed a facelift; many of the buildings had not been touched since they were built nearly a century before. The Central Building, for example, was one of the very first buildings completed in 1878; in 1960 work began on its complete restoration and redecoration, and it was re-opened two years later as the new Somerville-Weir Hall, to seat 500. The cottages were thoroughly modernised and repaired – work which had been going on, too, during the late 1950s. The dormitories were made more homely and comfortable, with carpets on the floors, bright bedspreads, small personal bedside tables and lockers, and the children's own pictures and posters on the walls. Downstairs the kitchens gradually acquired more mod-cons, with modern cookers replacing the old black open ranges.

The children got their own swimming pool, opened in 1966 by the Scottish Olympic champion swimmer, Bobby Macgregor. A brand-new recreation centre was built two years later. On the site of the old training ship for boys, the *James Arthur*, a tuckshop was built where the children could spend their pocket money and lay in supplies of sweets for the week.

Outside the Quarrier's Homes complex there were other changes. The City Home at James Morrison Street, which Quarrier had opened in 1876, and which for many years had been a home for working boys in the city, had been sold in 1937. But this was not the end of the Working Boys' Hostel; the boys, about twenty of them, were moved to new premises at 1 Dumbreck Road, on Glasgow's south side, and a new hostel was established there in a house called Overbridge. It was converted into a children's home in 1965 and a few years later it was relocated to St Andrew's Drive in Pollockshields, where it continued to look after children until 1985.

Quarrier's Homes also kept up the long association with the Firth of Clyde coast which began in the 1920s when parties of children were sent to various houses in Dunoon and the surrounding area for their summer holidays. During the 1960s children spent the summer weeks in a holiday house in Girvan, a seaside resort south of Ayr. Not far from Girvan, on the estates of the wealthy industrialist, Mr Niall Hodge, the Homes also had the use of several holiday cottages. Until his death in July 1981, Mr Hodge kept very close links with the Homes and gave generously of his time and money to make the cottages at Turnberry a marvellous resort for the children.

But the changes which really affected the fabric of life in Quarrier's Homes for the children and staff during this period took place within the cottages. The arrival of a new Superintendent started the ball rolling. After twenty-four years as Superintendent of the children at Bridge of Weir, Mr Hector Munro retired in 1963 and his place was taken by Mr Roy Holman from London. One of the first things Mr Holman did on his arrival was to start mixing boys and girls in the cottages. This had been started rather tentatively with the toddlers after the war, but even

Having fun in the Homes' swimming pool

in the 1960s the majority of children still lived in segregated cottages, often separated from their brothers and sisters.

In 1965 Roy Holman returned to London, and an Aberdonian, Mr Joseph Mortimer, joined Quarrier's Homes as Superintendent and Deputy General Director, bringing with him highly professional credentials – he was one of the first male holders of the Certificate of Social Studies from Edinburgh University. He consolidated much of the work done by Roy Holman and introduced many more changes, improvements and new approaches to the work of the Homes.

One of his main areas of concern was the training of staff. Traditionally, residential childcare workers had always lagged behind field workers in professional training. Residential work with children had been considered as something which could hardly be learned; the only 'qualifications' needed, it was thought, were things like common sense and the ability to understand children and run a house. Many men and women who had spent perhaps twenty years in the job were unimpressed by the argument that a more formal training would help them in any way with their job. Up to that point Quarrier's Homes had been more concerned that their staff should profess a Christian faith and be committed to the ethos and traditions at Bridge of Weir than that they should have professional qualifications. But Joe Mortimer knew that the Homes' house-parents would have to be able to hold their own in the fast-changing, professional world of childcare, with its increasing demands upon those to whom other people's children had been entrusted. He began to second some of his staff to childcare and social studies courses all over the country, and, with his assistant, Mr William Dunbar, devised new in-service training courses to replace those which had been going on in a desultory way since the 1950s. One day a week cottage parents from the Homes, and other people from outside the village with a specific interest in childcare matters, attended lectures and seminars on such subjects as child development, the problem of adolescence, the health of children and the importance of leisure time and how best to use it for the benefit of the children.

It was also during this period that the foundations of a social work unit within the Homes were laid. The social workers provided much-needed support and back-up for cottage-mothers and -fathers. It was becoming obvious that looking after fifteen or twenty children under one roof was a mammoth task for anyone and that more staff were needed in every cottage. Staffing levels were gradually increased and by the early 1980s each cottage had either a cottage-mother and -father plus four assistant house-parents, or a cottage-mother with five assistant house-parents, all working on a rota basis. There was also a cottage manager who was put in charge of the smooth general running of a group of cottages.

Children in the Homes from the 1960s onwards enjoyed a very different lifestyle from their predecessors. They had more freedom to come and go, to visit Bridge of Weir and Glasgow at weekends, to go on group outings and mix freely with children from other cottages. However, it was still a sheltered environment, especially for those children spending years there from a young age. Far away from the city, this strange Village of children was beautifully situated, free from pollution and heavy traffic, with wide tree-lined avenues and pleasant views. It was all so pleasantly rural that Elizabeth McLean, who spent several years at the Homes in the 1960s, got quite a shock when she returned to the city:

> The one problem I had when I left was getting used to traffic on the roads. When we were in Quarrier's there were no cars or very few that went through the Village, and to come and stay in a busy town was quite frightening for the first few weeks.

Increasing access to the outside world minimised the problems of isolation, but there was also the problem of educating the children in the use of money. At that time everything necessary simply fell at their feet like manna from heaven. The store within the Homes had everything for the cottage, and cottage-mothers simply filled in a form for what they wanted, handed it in at the counter and walked away with the provisions. The drapery provided for all the clothing needs of the children and issued them with skirts, blouses, trousers and other articles whenever they were needed. The brown three-wheeled bread van came around the cottages every morning, and milk from the nearby dairy was delivered to each doorstep. Joe Mortimer felt that it would benefit the children to be educated a little in the realities of money and what it could buy, so he introduced a clothing allowance for fifth formers and above, which enabled them to buy clothes outwith the village or, if they wanted, buy priced articles at the drapery store. However they used the allowance, it was up to them to make it last and to budget accordingly. A hairdressing allowance was introduced for the girls so that they could go into Bridge of Weir if they wanted rather than standing in line with dozens of others for the free cuts given by a visiting hairdresser, who regularly came to the Village. And instead of a small amount of pocket money supplemented by 'free issues' of so many sweets or so many comics per week for each child, the amount of pocket money was increased to enable the children to make the choices themselves.

The Quarrier's children were given a voice to express their needs and wishes; in 1967 Joe Mortimer held the first meeting of the Boys' and Girls' Council, at which children from all the cottages discussed questions and suggestions about Village life from their point of view. This was ahead of its time: it wasn't until 1975 that the National Children's Bureau launched their *Who Cares?* campaign with a book written by children in care about what it was like to be in care.

But for two people, at least, the most important change for the better at the Homes was neither the clothing allowance nor the Council,

The Boys' and Girls' Council with Mr Mortimer

but the introduction of alternatives to the cottage for older children as part of the gradual progression towards independent living outside the Homes. Many hundreds of former Boys and Girls who lived at Bridge of Weir in the days when you were more or less turned loose and abandoned to the big wide world once your time was up would sympathise with the sentiments of Catharine Hopkins and David Wilson. Catharine keenly remembered the nightmare of the day she left Quarrier's Homes in 1920 – the day after she had been informed by the Matron that she was leaving. She had never been out of the Homes on her own before; yet she was taken to Bridge of Weir station and simply told to get the train to Glasgow. She was seventeen, and she didn't even know where Glasgow was. And so she sat in the train and cried all the way, ignored by all the other passengers.

David Wilson at least had the advantage of having made a trial journey on his own into Glasgow before he left the Homes in 1956; but he describes that practice day as 'the most traumatic experience I had':

> When the great day arrived, I was terrified. I got the bus to Bridge of Weir station. The first train was for Glasgow, but by the time it arrived at Paisley I had had enough. Off I got and as I stood outside the station, thinking, 'What shall I do?', the first place I saw was a cinema. In I went. The movie was *Carousel*, my very first movie. Afterwards, straight home – boy, was I glad!

Children were simply not prepared for the shock of leaving the cottage and the shelter of this isolated, enclosed community. Although in the old days they were far better able to look after themselves physically (they could cook, clean, sew), for many the discovery of all the complications and unfamiliarities of the environment outside the village was tremendously hard. They knew nothing of the ways of the world, they had had no training in the use of money, and there had been no intermediate stage to soften the blow between cottage life (lived wholly inside the Village) and life outside. All that began to change in 1970 when one of the cottages in the Village was converted into a hostel for older boys and girls of fifteen and over, where they could live a little more independently (although under supervision) rather than being looked after by cottage parents. The following year, as part of the centenary celebrations of the founding of the first Home in Glasgow, Quarrier's Former Boys and Girls Association donated the cost of an extension to the cottage. The next stage on from the supervised hostel was a smaller, unsupervised bed-sit unit where half a dozen boys and girls had to do their own cooking, buy their own food and look after themselves. By that time some of them might have a job outside the Village; by living within the Homes they still had contact with their familiar environment for support and help, but were learning how to live independently. The final stage on this path to independence was one of Quarrier's five flats in nearby Foxbar, Paisley, which the Homes sub-let to their teenagers when they were ready to move out of the Village.

Once it recognised the problems older children could face when they had to leave Bridge of Weir after years in care, Quarrier's Homes tried hard to help them to adjust to independent living and some of the group projects they developed for their teenagers in the late '70s and early '80s were extremely valuable. By then, however, there was a far greater challenge for the organisation looming on the horizon, a challenge which was not about helping children to leave the Homes: it was about coping with the realisation that fewer and fewer children would be coming into the Homes in the first place. The world had changed and Quarrier's Homes had to change with it.

Chapter 11

Crisis

Far away in the northeast corner of India the town of Kalimpong looks out towards Tibet beyond the snow-covered peaks of the Himalayas. There, in 1900, Dr John Graham, a Church of Scotland missionary, had founded a community of cottage Homes for the hundreds of poor and abandoned Anglo-Indian children he saw every day in the tea plantations he visited on his missionary travels through the country.

Dr Graham's Homes in Kalimpong are part of the Quarriers story. The doctor had modelled the entire complex, right down to the design of the cottages, on the Orphan Homes of Scotland, which he had visited at the end of the 1890s. Moreover, Dr James Minto, who joined Quarrier's Homes as General Director and successor to Dr Romanes Davidson in 1974, was Principal of the Kalimpong Homes from 1958 until 1971.

Dr Minto took up his new post as General Director at a time when change was very definitely in the air; indeed, in his inaugural Annual General Meeting address he spoke of the 'winds of change' which were beginning to blow around the Homes. A shift in the balance of the relationship between the Homes and the local authorities was becoming evident. During the 1960s the Homes had been financially secure and more or less independent, but by the 1970s they were more and more reliant upon the maintenance grants which came with each child referred to the Homes by the local authority. It became clear to Dr Minto that, in future, Quarrier's Homes would have to work much more closely with the statutory authorities and fall in with their ideas and plans for the care of children.

These plans did not favour the set-up at Bridge of Weir. As late as the 1960s this model Village, set in pleasant surroundings deep in the Renfrewshire countryside where 500 children lived, worked and played, was apparently still acceptable to developing childcare theories. But by the 1970s, after the new social work departments had been formed with wide-ranging powers to help children in their natural families, this kind of residential care was regarded as old-fashioned. Local authorities did not approve of an isolated complex of cottages where the children led lives usually far removed from the kind of life they came from and to which they would return. Social workers looked with suspicion on a self-contained community from which the children seldom ventured, even to go to school: right up until 1980, when the boys and girls were enrolled at many different schools in the Port Glasgow and Greenock area, all the children were educated at their own William Quarrier School within the Homes' grounds.

Dr Minto held discussions with the local authorities and soon realised that the way forward for the Homes lay in joint projects outwith the Village complex. The Homes already had three outposts – small residential children's homes outside the Village. These were Overbridge in Glasgow, Merton in Largs and another small residential home in Girvan – Seabank – to which some of the more intellectually gifted children from Bridge of Weir were transferred for enrolment in schools in the neighbourhood. Now came two entirely new projects outside the Village, conceived, funded and carried out jointly with the local authorities: an Intermediate Treatment Centre (IT) and a residential unit for children with emotional and behavioural problems.

The IT Centre at Yonderton (near Glasgow Airport) was begun in 1975 and was a continuation of pioneering work started at Turnberry as far back as 1966. Operating both on a farm at West Yonderton and in the children's neighbourhoods, the project offered community-based support to youngsters and teenagers in difficulty, through group work, discussions and continuous liaison with local social workers.

Southannan, at Fairlie, near Largs, opened in 1978 as what was then described as a List G residential unit for maladjusted and disturbed youngsters, and was the first of its kind in Scotland. Social workers had been looking extremely closely at residential childcare since the early 1970s and in the report *Home or Away? Residential Childcare Strategy for the Eighties*, Strathclyde Region Social Work Department had made clear its intentions to broaden the range of residential care services which were available for children and to work more closely with voluntary agencies in developing more specialist services. Southannan was an example of that new collaboration and, indeed, was singled out in the report as an example of the work being undertaken by some voluntary childcare organisations.

Strathclyde Region was born on 16 May 1975. It was a very important day for Quarrier's Homes because the creation (under the 1973 Local Government (Scotland) Act) of this huge new regional authority was to have a direct effect on the numbers of children in the Village. Strathclyde had a population of 2,250,000 people and was the region for west central Scotland, stretching from Skye to the Clyde and from Renfrewshire to Lanarkshire. It comprised twenty-two former counties, including Ayrshire, Dunbartonshire, Bute, most of Argyll

Southannan residential unit at Fairlie, near Largs

and part of Stirlingshire. With its enormous budget, extensive powers and well-defined policies, the Social Work Department of the new region made its presence felt immediately in the area of childcare. Its policies were clear: children were first and foremost to be kept in their own homes and supported within the community if at all possible. Community care was the ideal to be aimed at. What this involved was discussed in a report by the Officer/Member group of the region's Social Work Committee, entitled *Room to Grow* (1978). It defined community care as:

Any action, initiative, provision or policy which enables children to remain with their families in their own community.

The new region had the money to finance projects such as nursery schools, play groups and day-care centres. Social workers could work closely with, for example, housing departments to help avoid the accumulation of rent arrears which so often in the past had resulted in eviction and the children having to go into care. Or, as the report suggested, the region could develop a scheme whereby a number of peripatetic house-parents could temporarily look after children in their own home, if, for example, the mother were in hospital – another common reason for children being placed in care. However, if a child had to be taken from, or could not live with, its natural parents, Strathclyde advocated fostering or adoption as the next best thing. Accordingly, very soon after its creation, the region launched a massive fostering campaign and tried to get as many children out of residential care as possible. They wanted everyone to be in on it, local authority homes as well as voluntary ones, and Quarrier's Homes were quick to respond. In 1977 they embarked upon the Quarrier's Family Fostering Project, a joint scheme in which they worked closely with Strathclyde social workers and successfully fostered about fifty of their children, many of whom had been in the Homes for years.

Strathclyde region was still committed to retaining the option of residential care if fostering were not possible, but it wanted the units to be more specialised; the *Home or Away?* report highlighted 'residential rehabilitation and residential treatment and control' as key areas, and also noted that:

the type of unit designed to help young people to move towards independent living in the community is likely to be the greatest aspect of residential care in the future.

The region still had a need for residential care, but during the 1970s it began to use its own homes more and more in preference to those in the voluntary sector. All these factors – community care, fostering and adoption and changing trends in residential care – plus the dramatic drop in the birthrate from the late 1960s onwards, were reflected in the decreasing numbers of children in Quarrier's Homes. There were nearly 500 children when Dr Minto joined in 1974, of whom about seventy-five were babies and toddlers. In 1978, the centenary year of the establishment of the Homes at Bridge of Weir, there were still nearly 400 children, although Dr Minto referred in his Annual Report to expert opinion in childcare which predicted that there would never again be the same numbers of children in residential care. However, the Homes did not seem unduly worried; they felt quite secure in the knowledge that their cottages were full and that so far the decrease in numbers had been slow and steady.

But suddenly the unthinkable happened – almost overnight, it seemed. At the beginning of 1980, Quarrier's Homes were looking after more than 300 children; but by December 1980, only three months into the new financial year, they had fifty fewer children than were needed to cover the organisation's costs. When Strathclyde Region made it clear that the numbers would not be made up, the Homes realised they were facing a crisis.

How had it happened? In the long term the region's policies and the fall in the birth rate had taken their toll of the numbers; but the sudden and dramatic drop in admissions was a result of something quite different: Strathclyde had been putting its own house in order. A computer was installed in their headquarters in 1980 which rationalised the whole network of children's homes and the number of places available in the region. Strathclyde discovered that they could accommodate far more children in their own homes than they had been doing. Consequently, at a time when they were also closing some of their own homes because of falling numbers and financial stringency, they were anxious not to fill up voluntary places at the expense of their own.

Quarrier's Homes can hardly be blamed for being caught short, because the decrease was so sudden. At a meeting with Strathclyde officials as late as June 1980, just six months before the blow fell, the region had not made it clear that the numbers of children they would be referring for the next financial year would be insufficient to cover the Homes' costs. On the other hand, all that Strathclyde was really doing was forcing the pace, dealing quickly the blow which was bound to come anyway. In reality Quarrier's Homes had, for many years, been out on a limb in terms of residential childcare in Scotland, still providing for hundreds of children at a time when all other Homes were for small groups; still improving and expanding the Village complex (a new sports centre was added in 1977) many years after similar large voluntary organisations like Barnardo's Homes and Aberlour Children's Homes (now the Aberlour Child Care Trust) had run down their Villages and diversified into smaller, specialist units all over the country. The time to change was the late 1960s and early 1970s as Barnardo's and Aberlour had done, at a time when Quarrier's Homes had plenty of money and could have ploughed it into areas of specialist care, smaller satellite units, care for men and women with disabilities, the elderly or any other groups with which the local authorities could not cope. But Quarrier's Homes missed the boat.

In a way, though, even if the Homes had been as aware as they should have been of the changing climate of childcare, even if they had been forward-thinking enough to see the day when there would no longer be a need for their huge residential complex, and had decided that the Village should be run down and the services diversified, that awareness would not have been much use, because the Homes' best qualities and most enduring traditions would have been their worst enemies. Running down the Village and looking positively into different kinds of care for the future would have meant saying to the local authorities, 'We shall take no more children'; Quarrier's Homes, with its cherished tradition of helping any child in need, would never have done that and did not do so in the 1970s either. It would have meant, as it did for Barnardo's and Aberlour, adopting a more businesslike and professional attitude to money by advertising for funds and support for new ventures – and this, too, the traditions of the Homes would not have allowed. Quarrier's Homes had never made a public appeal for money, and it seems that there was no one in the organisation who saw the need or was willing to break with these traditions.

Instead, they carried on as usual. It was all too easy to assume that all would be well but, when the emergency came, the effect was devastating. At a crisis board meeting in December 1980 the cold facts had to be faced: fifty vacancies, fifty local authority maintenance grants to be deducted from income, a resultant overdraft of £250,000, the prospect of a working loss for the year of £400,000 and the imminent closure of cottages and redundancies for large numbers of staff.

By the time of the next board meeting in March 1981 Strathclyde Region had informed Dr Minto that the Homes would never again receive the same numbers of children. It was clear that Quarrier's Homes could no longer be the organisation it had been; caring for children could no longer be their life's work as it had been for more than a hundred years.

Chapter 12

The End of an Era

Could Quarrier's Homes now survive and, if so, how? In the anxious early months of 1981, as cottages closed and staff were made redundant, these were the questions facing Dr Minto and the Board of Management. The grim situation confronting them – rapidly decreasing numbers of children and the threat of financial collapse – demanded positive and radical action. Somehow they had to re-organise Quarrier's Homes without children into a useful, viable voluntary agency with something to offer Scotland in the 1980s and beyond.

What they came up with was a bold scheme to create a completely new community at Bridge of Weir – to change Quarrier's Homes into Quarrier's Village. In June 1982 Dr Minto presented his Eight-Year Plan to the Board, a phased strategy to change and develop the organisation's services and thereby to ensure its financial survival. The idea was to use the rapidly emptying cottages to support other vulnerable and needy groups like the elderly and people with a disability; to lease other buildings to small industries and businesses; to act as landlord to various caring organisations, and to finance it all by selling tracts of adjoining land and the remaining cottages for commercial housing development.

The Eight-Year Plan was a scheme born out of dire financial necessity, but Dr Minto and the Board passionately believed that they could create something lasting and valuable which would continue the caring work of the organisation in a new kind of community. As

Residents and staff at Fountainview enjoying a musical break

the numbers of children continued to fall, this strange, new Village took shape. In April 1984 there were about ninety children living in cottages and another twenty-two in bedsit and hostel units. In 1985 that number was down to seventy, in the following year forty-eight, then twenty, until, in 1989, just one child remained in Quarrier's Village. Their places were being taken by other people who needed the support and care which the organisation had been providing for well over a century. Campbell-Maltman Home, which used to be full of toddlers and babies, was converted into a Respite Care Unit for children and adults with physical and learning disabilities.

Other cottages in the Village were given over to the care of men and women with learning disabilities who had previously spent most of their lives in large institutions like Lennox Castle, a huge, Victorian, long-stay hospital near the Campsie Hills north of Glasgow. Quarrier's Village also leased two cottages to the Abbeyfield Society, a national charitable organisation which provides sheltered accommodation for elderly men and women, and sold the old Elise Hospital building to the Masonic Order for conversion to retirement flats.

Several cottages were leased to other care groups, including KIND (Kids in Need and Distress), a Liverpool-based voluntary organisation providing activity holidays in the country for children from the city. Women's Aid also rented a cottage in the Village, which remained in use as a refuge until 1997.

The biggest danger in filling up the empty cottages with different groups of people needing support was that it was still compounding the problem of being an artificial community out on a limb, a large caring institution in the middle of nowhere. So Dr Minto and the Board sold eleven acres of land all around the Village to Barratt Urban Renewal (Scotland) Ltd and Barratt (Glasgow) Ltd for commercial development, and put well over a dozen cottages on the open market; they hoped that, as well as raising much-needed cash, introducing private housing into the Village would also achieve a better balance and create a more 'normal' living environment. By 1988, in addition to the private houses and flats and the care services, this unlikely Village had a coffee house, a craft centre, a Village shop, thirteen small industries and businesses, a library and a post office. To some extent these measures stabilised the organisation's finances in the short term, and Quarrier's Village started to develop some new, progressive projects outside the Village, including a Family Centre in an area of high urban deprivation in Greenock.

This was the new Quarriers (the 'Village' and the apostrophe were gradually dropped from the name) which Dr Minto left on his retirement in 1990. The speech he delivered to the 119th Annual General Meeting in Mount Zion Church was honest and heartfelt:

> I would be a hypocrite if I did not admit I have enjoyed the challenge of helping to guide Quarriers through the minefield of change. In fact I have personally enjoyed my last ten years in Quarriers much more than, say, my first seven years: The professional criticism of the pre-1981 Quarriers was vociferous and meant that whenever I was attending a conference or meeting outside the Village my response had always to be defensive about the Village. Five hundred children looked after in a protected environment, no matter how beautiful, attending the same school and where most of the children even went on their cottage holidays together to Turnberry, could never be totally right. It should be said, however, that for some children the system worked well; but for others it could not produce the stimulating atmosphere of healthy competition and sound preparation for survival for the time when the children came out of care. Having said this, the change, when it did come, was too drastic, too sudden . . . The changes for you former Girls and Boys were understandably harder to take than most. I completely understand your bewilderment at the speed and direction of change. The Village you grew up in is no more and that in itself is hard to take. It has, however, been replaced by an equally fascinating Village with a wide caring base and I know that many of you now have a better understanding of what has been achieved . . . The last ten years have been exhilarating as a changed Quarriers has risen from the old.

Dr Minto died on 8 April 1995, on the eve of his sixty-ninth birthday. He was a well-liked man who is remembered affectionately by many people in the Village, not just for himself but because he fought so hard for the survival of the organisation he loved. He believed in the Village of the Eight-Year Plan, and he and his team worked tirelessly in their efforts to turn around the fortunes of the organisation and to try to secure for it some kind of future at the end of the 1980s. However, that future remained both financially precarious and professionally uncertain. Great waves of change in social care theory and practice were still breaking all around the Village as they had been during the 1980s, and although Quarriers had weathered the immediate financial storm by the short-term measures of closing cottages and selling off assets, they were still struggling against the tide professionally. Caring for people in their communities and homes, rather than in institutions, hospitals and places set apart, had been the impetus behind social care policy for some time, and the NHS and Community Care Act 1990 enshrined this in law. Quarriers had taken some significant steps towards embracing the new ideas with projects such as the Larkfield Family Centre in Greenock, and they were continuing to provide care for men and women who had come back into the community from long-stay mental hospitals like Lennox Castle. Southannan in Ayrshire was still doing valuable work with young people with emotional and behavioural difficulties. The main focus of the Eight-Year Plan, however, had always been inwards to the Village, not outwards to the wider world. This needed to change for the new business of caring in the 1990s. The survival of Quarriers, and its future as a professionally respected voluntary organisation, depended on it.

Chapter 13

Tackling Change

The 1990s saw many changes at Quarriers. Several key people who had given long service decided that the time had come to hand over the reins to a new team. Joe Mortimer, the Deputy General Director and a man with more than twenty years in the organisation, retired in 1991; Mr W.H. Hunter, who had taken over from Viscount Muirshiel as Chairman of the Council of Management in 1990, handed over the following year to Sir Graham Hills, formerly the Principal of Strathclyde University; and over the next year or so many long-standing council members with years of devoted service to Quarriers stood down to make way for new members.

The main change, however, was the appointment of a new General Director. Dr Minto had retired in 1990 and John Rea, previously the Scottish Director of Barnardo's, took the helm for fourteen months before handing over to his Director of Social Work and Depute Director, Gerald Lee. When he became General Director in July 1993 (later re-named Chief Executive), Gerald Lee inherited an organisation with a proud and unique tradition of caring which needed to be radically re-organised and re-energised for the future. He and his new management team became responsible for a large number of community-based services and a village complex which consisted of a mixture of private homes, a few small businesses, care services provided by Quarriers and others, and many additional buildings, some of which were empty and others which were in danger of falling into disrepair.

At this point Quarriers still cared for children in two cottages, one with a house-mother in the old tradition, and the other staffed by careworkers working shifts, looking after sibling groups who could not be fostered. Quarriers continued to provide this service for another few years until local government re-organisation in 1996. Glasgow City Council decided, as Strathclyde Region had done more than a decade before, that it could no longer afford to send these children to Bridge of Weir and that it should be providing for them within the geographical boundaries of its own social work area. Quarriers was given three months' notice and had to lay off staff at the children's cottages.

There was an enormous amount to be done in those early years of the 1990s, both in improving existing services and creating new ones. One long-established area which was in particular need of attention was the Epilepsy Centre, the last of William Quarrier's great pioneering works for Scotland. The first cottage for thirty men had opened in 1906, two years after Quarrier's death, and the operation had grown rapidly over the years.

Epilepsy is the most common serious neurological disorder affecting people of all ages and backgrounds – around 1 in 200 of the population, perhaps 40,000 people in Scotland alone; yet among the general population, awareness and understanding remain at a low level. The effects of epilepsy can vary from occasional and minor disturbances of normal life to a severe and totally disabling condition profoundly affecting the lives of sufferers and their families. In William Quarrier's day there was little understanding of the condition and virtually nothing in the way of medical treatment. The thirty men who lived in the early Colony were simply looked after in dormitories and given plenty of fresh air, light work and exercise. The charge at the time was 10s 6d a week which, for most colonists, as they were called, was paid by friends and relatives or the parish council.

The Colony grew rapidly and by 1933 consisted of four accommodation buildings and a workshop. During the 1940s and 1950s things became rather cramped, with more admissions all the time but no more beds, so several cottages in the children's Village were turned into small epilepsy units, mostly for boys. Life went on very much in the same way for the men and women at the Epilepsy Centre: they worked all day in the workshop or the gardens or the kitchens,

*One of Quarriers' trainees ready to serve at the salad bar in Somerville's
Restaurant, in Quarriers Village*

they retired to their cottages at night. The great majority had been doing this for many years and there seemed no hope that they would ever be doing anything else, because the Centre had, like the Homes during the first half of the century, settled into institutional rigidity: there were increasing numbers of people not just with epilepsy but with other physical and mental disabilities and, with a growing army of medical staff caring for them night and day, it was inevitable that the Centre became, in effect, a long-stay hospital, cut off from the modern world by the big iron gates at the entrance to the main drive which were closed each night.

It was clear that the Centre had to be pulled into the modern world. A number of changes were made in the 1970s in an effort to de-institutionalise the service. History repeated itself when Dr Minto went to the Chalfont Centre in Buckinghamshire, the first place which William Quarrier had visited at the turn of the century when he was planning his own Colony. The Centre was being run by a Scot from Edinburgh, Dr John Laidlaw, who was working towards rehabilitation into the outside world for residents and he had begun to admit residents to Chalfont for assessment and treatment.

Dr Minto came back from Chalfont with many ideas and plans for improving the quality of life for residents and staff at the re-named Epilepsy Centre at Quarrier's Homes and over the next few years new accommodation units were built to replace the huge Victorian dormitories. A Rehabilitation Officer was appointed for the first time, and in 1979 Dr John Laidlaw of Chalfont became the new Chief Consultant. He replaced nursing staff with care staff in the residential units in an attempt to normalise the environment. He also substantially reduced and controlled the number of very powerful anti-convulsant drugs which were being prescribed, and drove forward the short-term admissions and assessment work.

In the early 1990s the Epilepsy Centre consisted of 140 men and women with epilepsy living at the Centre or in cottages in the Village, and an assessment unit providing a unique national service. But, in common with some other areas of Quarriers' work at this time, the Centre still lagged behind current developments in social care, both philosophically and professionally. The Community Care Act of 1990 had transformed standards and aspirations for organisations, like

Quarriers, who were providing residential services for adults with disabilities or chronic health problems. Although great improvements had been made, there was still an institutional character to some of the accommodation in the Epilepsy Centre and conditions were too similar to those which existed in the long-stay hospitals around the country where closure programmes had already begun. Due to lack of adequate funding from the local authorities the Epilepsy Centre, under the leadership of Dr Jane Gray, had an uphill struggle to make changes in the physical environment or to achieve the staffing levels required.

The breakthrough came in 1994 when Gerald Lee commissioned a report on the Centre from TACT (Thames and Chiltern Trust), a well-respected organisation which had experience of similar long-stay hospitals in England. The report was critical and pulled no punches in its assessment of how the needs of residents at Bridge of Weir were being met. It was clear to the local authorities that they needed radically to improve funding for the service so that it could be developed in line with modern thinking.

From that point onwards the drive was to de-institutionalise the services for people with epilepsy and to bring the Centre right up-to-date in its approach, its staffing levels and its standards of care. New residential services for residents both in the Village and outside in the community were developed, and in 2001 the central administration block and Lawview were closed and demolished. During the 1990s Hunter House, Quarriers' epilepsy assessment unit, consolidated its reputation as a unique centre of expertise: it is still the only residential assessment centre for complex forms of epilepsy in Scotland. As part of the overall revolution in the way in which Quarriers was financed during the 1990s the Centre was put on to a firm financial basis, so that health authorities not only referred patients to Hunter House for assessment but also paid for that service at a realistic level. Using technologies such as EEG and video-telemetry, today's expert staff at Hunter House, under Consultant Dr Maria Oto (who was appointed following the retirement of Dr Jane Gray in 2000), can fully explore the epileptic seizure or non-epileptic seizure pattern of patients and identify the correct treatment which will give them the best possible chance of managing their epilepsy when they return to their homes in the community.

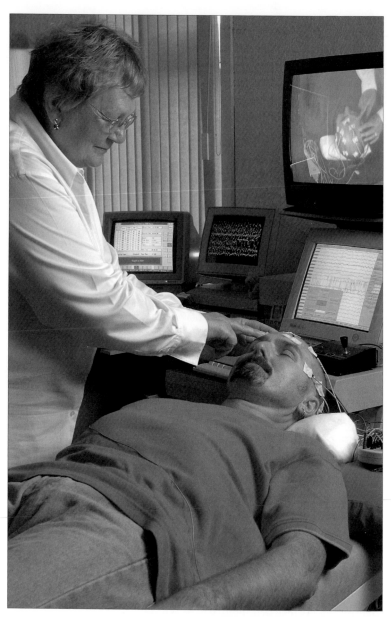

Patient wired up to the EEG machine in Hunter House, Scotland's national epilepsy monitoring unit in Quarriers Village

The re-assessment, modern thinking and new, realistic funding which helped transform the Epilepsy Centre in the 1990s were repeated across the whole Quarriers organisation. Gerald Lee's task was, through a mixure of reform, radical change and evolution, to equip Quarriers for the challenges and opportunities which the government's introduction of Care in the Community offered. Page four of the White Paper *Caring for People* (1990) set out the changes in the type and provision of care which were intended to:

> enable people to live as normal a life as possible in their own homes or in a homely environment in the local community;
>
> provide the right amount of care and support to help people achieve maximum possible independence and, by acquiring or reacquiring basic living skills, help them achieve their full potential;
>
> give people a greater individual say in how they lead their lives and the services they need to help them to do so.

Under the new arrangements the provision of this care was opened out to competition and the monopoly of the local authorities was broken up. Local authorities were charged with developing a new role as enablers, not sole direct providers, with a responsibility to identify and assess need, come up with a care package to meet that need and then find the most cost-effective way of delivering the care. And, most importantly for Quarriers and other private and voluntary agencies, the government laid a specific responsibility on local authorities to 'make increased use of non-statutory service providers' (White Paper p.23) for the delivery of care. The White Paper agreed with Sir Roy Griffiths' recommendations in his 1988 report *Community Care: Agenda for Action* that local authorities should develop an increasingly contractual relationship with voluntary bodies which would 'clarify the role of voluntary agencies' and 'give them a sounder financial base and allow them a greater degree of certainty in planning for the future' (White Paper p.24). This was the road Quarriers had to follow in the difficult years of the 1990s. The organisation had to forge a positive role for itself as a professionally up-to-date voluntary agency, in a new relationship with the local authorities, ready to tackle the multiple areas of need in the community wherever that community might be. The introduction to the 1991 Annual Report had set the compass for the road ahead:

Poverty, disability, hopelessness, isolation, discrimination, lack of choice or the opportunities most of us are able to take for granted – these are some of the distinguishing characteristics and experiences of the 800 children, families and adults Quarriers is working with today.

In such cases Quarriers is concerned in working with individuals and families in their community and through support networks and organisations to develop their special talents, help overcome adversity and realise their full potential.

And there was a very full account of the organisation's fund-raising and marketing strategy. The decision to break with tradition and allow direct appeals for money had been taken back in 1985, and a professional, dynamic fund-raising team was high on the priority list in 1991. Even higher, though, was the determination to put Quarriers on the map as a new organisation with a positive future:

It is hoped this report will help to scotch the myth that we are mainly about orphans growing up in residential homes in The Village at Bridge of Weir.

If anyone wasn't convinced by the end of 1991, the developments in the following years, under Gerald Lee, would change that. His goal was to transform the organisation in two central ways – financially and professionally. Gerald Lee described Quarriers' financial situation in 1992 as 'perilous': the turnover for that year was £5.2 million, but Quarriers was contributing £1.8 million of that from its own charitable reserves; in other words, the local authorities were not paying enough for the services which Quarriers was providing, Quarriers was not providing *enough* services and the organisation was haemorrhaging money to subsidise services, pay staff and maintain buildings and premises at Bridge of Weir. Simply continuing to sell off property and land in the Village – that is, the organisation's assets – was not a sustainable solution. A more sophisticated and detailed approach was necessary: in the contract culture of the 1990s between local authorities and care providers Quarriers needed to improve the training of staff and raise the organisation's professional profile; it needed to develop new projects and focus on the areas of care in which it could excel; and, crucially, Quarriers needed to cost its services properly and get out into the real world of competitive tenders and community-based projects.

Gerald Lee was not a man to approach the situation tentatively. He saw the need for radical action and forged ahead with what he judged to be the necessary changes. He brought in a new management team of young, highly qualified social work professionals and re-structured and re-named the various services into new areas of responsibility: Children, Families and Young People; Services for Men and Women with a Learning Disability; and Services for People with Epilepsy. Central to his vision was the need for better training and development of staff. There was no personnel department at that time so he established a Human Resources department which had a wide remit to support, train and develop staff through all the changes, to encourage and develop best professional practice, and to improve recruitment procedures. The central aim was to transform the organisational culture of Quarriers from a 125-year-old children's charity, built on solid foundations but bruised and buffeted by the events of the past decade, into a modern voluntary care agency, fit for purpose.

In its own way this period of change was as dramatic as any of the episodes in Quarriers' long history. It was not in the same mould as the colourful narrative of William Quarrier's life story, his rescue of street children, his creation of the Orphan Homes of Scotland, or his continual campaigning for the weak and wretched and ignored of society; but the 1990s were a crucial era in the history of Quarriers because those were the years when very difficult decisions had to be made, when the organisation had to take a long, hard look at itself and decide what it wanted to be, and when the old had to make way for the new.

There is no doubt that it was also an exciting time, especially for the new people in charge. There was a pioneering spirit, an urgency and a willingness to get stuck into the task in hand. Phil Robinson, who joined in 1992 as Assistant Director, Children, Families and Young People (and who has been Chief Executive of Quarriers since 2000), remembers sitting up all night writing policies on a range of childcare and employment issues (Quarriers at that time had hardly any written policies and procedures), drafting tenders for new services, devising projects and costing them down to the last pence and hour of staff time – something which Gerald Lee taught him from Day One. There was only one computer in the whole organisation at that time (actually just an Amstrad word processor) and budgets were prepared by the Director of Finance in longhand, in pencil, on a sheet of paper. 'And,' remembers Phil, 'you had to justify getting a new pencil, because there was no money!' Phil also did all the recruitment himself: he composed the adverts, placed them in the newspapers, wrote to the candidates, conducted the interviews. 'That was the kind of environment it was,' he remembers. 'We were, in a way, re-inventing this organisation. We worked very, very hard and it was very exciting.'

The hard work paid off. The negotiations over budgets for services were lengthy and complex but eventually resulted in significant increases in levels of funding. The local authorities recognised the long association they had with Quarriers and were encouraged by Quarriers' plans for change and development. The higher levels of funding meant that previously under-funded and poorly staffed services could be given a new injection of life.

As finances began to stabilise during the mid-1990s the new management team turned its attention to the areas of need the charity was addressing, the kind of support it offered and the projects it was running. This was the point at which the focus of Quarriers, which for more than a hundred years had been directed inwards to the Village, now began to move resolutely outwards to cities, towns and communities all over Scotland. Whereas William Quarrier had begun his work in the heart of Victorian Glasgow and then moved to the rural peace of Bridge of Weir, the modern organisation knew it had to do the opposite: the future lay beyond the Village.

Chapter 14

Beyond the Village

Quarriers Village, Bridge of Weir, looks much the same as it did twenty, even fifty, years ago. Large sandstone cottages still line the wide avenues which are fringed by sycamore and beech trees. Mount Zion church still towers above the rooftops of buildings which have stood since 1878 when William Quarrier brought the first trainload of orphaned children from the streets of Glasgow to this beautiful rural corner of Renfrewshire. In reality, though, the place has changed dramatically over the last fifteen years. What Quarriers does, and where and how it does it, is different from what it traditionally was – and the process of evolution is still going on.

In fact, there are many physical changes to the Village which are evident on closer inspection. Three-quarters of the original children's cottages and other buildings are owned by private householders, small businesses and commercial agencies. 'Homelea', the house where William Quarrier and his family lived, is no longer the head office for Quarriers: since the 1990s that has been located in 'Laing-Shrewsbury', which was originally a cottage for babies and toddlers. Next door is 'Campbell-Maltman' which, in the 1980s, was a respite care unit for severely disabled children and young adults; it has been converted to a staff training centre known as The Gateway. The centre was opened in 2003 by Cathy Jamieson, who was then the Minister for Children in the Scottish government. High-quality respite care is still being provided in the Village in Countryview children's respite unit, opened in 1997, which takes children aged five to eighteen who have a severe or profound learning disability. The average stay is for three or four days every month. In other locations all over the country Quarriers is directly supporting hundreds and hundreds of carers through care centres, support groups and respite projects.

Mount Zion church still stands at the heart of the Village but, like so many other church buildings in Scotland, it has been underused for years. Long gone are the days when thousands of children and adults gathered and worshipped there every week. Quarriers decided that it could no longer afford the upkeep of a Listed Building, and Mount Zion has been sold to a developer who specialises in restoring historic buildings. The plan is to convert the church into apartments, whilst keeping the external fabric almost untouched. The sale was subject to planning permission, which was finally granted in April 2006. This plan was greeted with anger by some former Boys and Girls who remember Mount Zion with great affection, and a group of them mounted a campaign to save the church – but to no avail.

Quarriers has promised that any proceeds from the sale will be used to provide enhanced facilities for the congregation (which currently worships in the old Bethesda building) and the Village community. The physical face of the Village will continue to change as Quarriers continues its evolution from a Victorian 'children's city' in the Renfrewshire countryside to the 'care village' of the 1980s and on to a modern voluntary care organisation (the third largest in Scotland) which runs more than eighty projects across Scotland.

The present Chief Executive, Phil Robinson, who took over from Gerald Lee in 2000, has continued the drive to modernise the organisation and re-focus its caring work; but having been with Quarriers since 1992 he has a deep regard for its past values and tradition of childcare. He is well aware that an organisation is built on people and that Quarriers had a very strong identity in the past which its staff and former Girls and Boys – and the Scottish charity-giving public – hold dear. It was a charity for children, an organisation founded, in an era of appalling social need and great philanthropy, on Christian principles which were a core part of its philosophy. It never publicly asked for money and many of its staff were people who had grown up there as children. Quarriers was their life. And then the

Enjoying a visit from the family at Rivendell residential unit for children and young people with complex needs

Phil Robinson, Chief Executive of Quarriers

world changed and the organisation had to change with it – or cease to exist. Phil Robinson knows how difficult these changes have been for some people to come to terms with, but he is convinced that this is all part of a process which William Quarrier himself would have embraced. He told me in a conversation in 2004:

> I like to think about how William Quarrier would operate in the modern era, having read a lot about the kinds of things he did and the stands he took. Of course, it's easy to kid yourself, and I can't claim the high moral ground, but I like to think he wouldn't be doing too much differently from what we're doing. Other people obviously disagree, for example over the sale of Mount Zion. Some people say, 'You've betrayed the legacy of William Quarrier. He'd be turning in his grave.' I honestly don't think so. I see him as a very pragmatic person whose values were about care for people in need. Christianity in practice, without walls. I don't think he had any allegiance to this place here generally, let alone the church building. I think he came here because this was how he could provide best for the children and if the time had come that he was convinced he could have provided better for the children somewhere else, he would just have sold up and gone. In a minute. I think that was the kind of guy he was, and that's what we try to be.

Of course, every leader of a long-established organisation likes to say he or she is in tune with the original founding spirit, but there is a sense in which the modern Quarriers is doing exactly as William Quarrier did: going out vigorously and positively into the world to care for people who are in most need, the people whom society doesn't value as it should. The fact that Quarriers is a twenty-first century care agency operating in a modern welfare state where the areas of need are very different from what they were in Victorian Scotland is beside the point: the spirit is the same.

The people Quarriers cares for are all over Scotland. The focus has shifted away from the Village as services were developed increasingly where people needed them most – in their own communities. Quarriers helps people who are homeless, gives family support, respite care and support for carers. It provides supported living for people with a disability, care in the community and help for disadvantaged young people in rural areas of Scotland.

The caring work covers three main areas: children, families and young people; people with a learning disability; and people with epilepsy. Quarriers runs a family centre in Greenock and a project in Oban

Lunchtime at Larkfield Family Centre in Greenock

called Oban Rooftops which provides support for young people who are renting their first flat.

One of the newest services is the Quarriers Family Resource Centre in Ruchazie, in the Easterhouse area of Glasgow. This project was created when Quarriers and Glasgow Social Work Department got together to talk about preventative work. The aim was to provide a service which would help families in crisis to stay together so that children would not have to come into care in the first place. Several other agencies became involved and a new Family Centre was built at a cost of £1.2 million. It has a tremendous record of success and a high profile in the care world. The Centre works with young parents (some of them who have come out of care themselves), single parents, parents with a drug and alcohol addiction and those involved in prostitution.

Youth homelessness is still a big area of concern for Quarriers and one project in particular, developed in the 1990s and still going strong, gives an insight into the modern organisation and its links with the past. Phil Robinson had just joined Quarriers as Director of Services for Young People when he developed Stopover in 1993. It was an existing project providing support for young homeless people, but it was being re-tendered by the council and Phil saw an opportunity for Quarriers. He told me how important this project was:

> This was our first venture back into youth homelessness, and we made a lot of that. We'd gone full circle. People in the business said, 'What does Quarriers know about youth homelessness? They don't know anything.' And we said, 'No, you're wrong. Our roots are in youth homelessness. We haven't done much in that area for a hundred years, but it's where we started.' So I made that link, saying, 'This is where William Quarrier started, rescuing children from the streets. Unfortunately it's needed again, and that's what we're doing, following in his footsteps.' And that's very powerful. And we meant it. We were very proud of what we were doing.

After more than a century, Quarriers was confronting the same acute social problem which had first galvanised William Quarrier into action. In his day, homelessness was everywhere in the teeming streets – the homelessness of the orphaned, the neglected and those in grinding poverty. In 1993/94 there were 42,800 homelessness applications in Scotland, 65 per cent of which were in Glasgow.* The root causes might have been different, but the need for help and support was the same.

Stopover opened in February 1995 in a refurbished tenement in the centre of Glasgow. (A new building has been built and will be opened in June 2006; the existing one lies in the path of the M74 extension.) It is a service for young homeless people in crisis who have many other problems in addition to their homelessness: some are fleeing from violence in the family home; some are the victims of physical and sexual abuse; many have a drug or alcohol dependency. This is a specialised unit which doesn't replicate existing services in Glasgow. The city is actually quite well-off for accommodation for the homeless

---

* Social Work Services Inspectorate figure

if all they need is a roof over their heads, but the young people coming to Stopover require much more. When they arrive they are allocated a key worker who works intensively with them for ten weeks, assessing their difficulties and aspirations, deciding what action to take. The key worker looks at their whole lifestyle, which includes employment, training and family, and talks through what they can do. The project's aim is to find out what the young people want and require so that they don't just end up back in the homelessness cycle. It's not easy. Ian Hughes (who now works at Quarriers head office) was the manager at Stopover at the beginning and he told me he had no illusions about the challenge of this type of work:

> I'm a pragmatist. We try and do the best we can for people while they're here. You can't measure success in relation to a young person's life by giving them a house, but what we can do is guarantee to move them on in most cases to a much safer address and if they require support we try to co-ordinate that for them.

There are many other projects for young people and families which Quarriers has developed over the years. It is a major part of the organisation's caring work, as are services for people with a learning disability. Quarriers runs projects in Glasgow, Ayrshire, Inverclyde, Renfrewshire, East Dunbartonshire and the Village at Bridge of Weir, and there is a growing demand for their services.

In the 1980s the learning disability services Quarriers ran were on the residential model, large hostels for ten or twelve men or women. Many such group-living units were set up by voluntary agencies and local authorities to accommodate large numbers of adults who were coming out of long-stay hospitals, as part of government policy to bring the elderly and people with a mental illness or disability out of institutional care. One of the principles behind working with learning disabled people is that, no matter how complex their difficulties or needs may be, they have the right to be supported in a home-like environment. One example of this is the Homelife Ayr project where seventeen people with very complex physical and learning disabilities are supported in their own homes. The adults live in different parts of South Ayrshire and staff travel to support and live with them, in shifts, round the clock. These are people who need intimate personal care, right through to assistance with eating. The project is about giving them the opportunities the rest of us take for granted, like going shopping, and also the chance to do things which might be considered risky, such as going on activity holidays. The point is that they are helped and supported in everything because, like everyone else, they are entitled to live their lives as fully as they can. Quarriers provides such person-centred services to hundreds of people with disabilities across the country.

In the early 1990s the priority at the Epilepsy Centre (now known today simply as The Upper Village) was to improve the living environments for residents and to develop systems called Personal Plans, which were part of modern social-work thinking but which were not in place at the Centre. A Personal Plan identifies someone's aspirations for his or her life and decides what sort of things have to be done to meet those aspirations. At one end of the scale, a Personal Plan might just be to have a room of one's own, or to learn how to cook a meal; at the other end, someone who is already able to live more independently might want to enrol at a night class and get a job. Whatever the plan, the service is then designed around that. It was part of the process of de-institutionalising the Epilepsy Centre and breaking everything down to make it smaller and more personal and to introduce, in social work jargon, 'ordinary-living models of care'.

The service fully embraced the Community Care injunction that people, no matter what their disability, should not be living in institutions but should be supported in their own home or community or whatever homely environment they choose. For some people who have lived at the Centre for thirty years, moving out into the wider community might not be what they want or feel able to cope with; Quarriers' pledge is to provide the highest-quality residential care for them. There will be many of them, because the residents are getting older. However, for others, moving away and living much more independently is very much on the cards, and Quarriers is supporting them in that, too.

For those people with epilepsy in the Village who don't want to move out into the community, Quarriers has set itself the task of providing the very highest standard of residential accommodation. The advent of the Care Commission in 2002 has meant that services are now divided

The Central Building, the first one built by William Quarrier, is now Somerville's, a restaurant and training facility for adults with learning disabilities who are supported by Quarriers

into two types: Registered Care Homes which are staffed around the clock and have the highest standards of accommodation, including lifts and en-suite facilities for every resident and lifts; and Housing Support Services which aim for the best possible standards of normal residential living, with support being provided externally according to the needs of the individual. Work continues on the conversion and renovation of properties in Quarriers Village to provide both types of accommodation for the remaining residents with epilepsy – and for adults with learning disabilities.

In 2000 Quarriers also took over responsibility for some Epilepsy Fieldwork Services in the north-east of Scotland which had previously been operated by the Epilepsy Association of Scotland (now Epilepsy Scotland). This was Quarriers' first venture into that part of Scotland and it has been a great opportunity to develop the organisation's reputation and profile, not only as a service provider but also through fundraising and other activities. Two pilot projects in Lanarkshire were also started – one a telephone helpline service for young people with epilepsy, and the other a scheme to provide epilepsy awareness and first-aid training for mainstream pupils in secondary schools. The aim was to reduce the stigma and fear which still surround the condition – nearly a century after William Quarrier first tried to make a positive impact in his own way, in his own time.

Quarriers has been making an impact in multiple areas of social need since those earliest days. What it does, and how well it does it, directly affects the lives of thousands of people in Scotland, young and old, able and disabled alike. The years of change which the organisation underwent were part of a process which will continue as long as Quarriers wants to be in the forefront of the voluntary care sector. As one of the oldest charities in Scotland, it has a long history to live up to – and, as Quarriers has found out in the last few years, that history had some dark aspects which the organisation has had to confront and come to terms with.

Chapter 15

Past Wrongs

Phil Robinson had been in his new post as Chief Executive for only a few weeks when he learned that a former Quarriers employee had been charged with abusing children in his care when he worked as a house-father in the Village in the 1960s. Eighteen months later, in September 2001, Samuel McBrearty was found guilty at the High Court in Glasgow of what the judge, Lord Reed, called 'appalling offences against some of the most vulnerable children'. He was convicted of repeatedly raping two girls and repeatedly indecently assaulting them and a third girl at Quarrier's Homes between 1961 and 1968. The girls were aged ten and twelve when the abuse began.

On the day the verdict was announced Quarriers held a press conference at which it acknowledged the awfulness of his crimes and expressed 'heartfelt sympathy' for his victims. The organisation knew that it had to be as open and honest as possible, partly because it was the right and proper thing to do but partly, too, because, by the time the Samuel McBrearty case came to trial, Quarriers had been informed that there were at least four other complaints against former staff being investigated: Samuel McBrearty was not a one-off case and Quarriers had to face up to the fact that this was just the beginning of a very difficult road.

Samuel McBrearty's trial and conviction (he was subsequently sentenced to twelve years in jail, later reduced to ten), and the news of allegations against other former staff, were a serious blow to Quarriers' public profile. Just when the organisation was emerging strongly from the years of financial struggle and professional evolution, here was a crisis which struck at the heart of the trusted commitment to caring which had been the foundation of Quarriers from its beginnings. The headlines in the newspapers pulled no punches: 'Orphans abused in Home that was hailed as a haven' (*Herald*, 8 September 2001); 'Sex monster's reign of abuse in orphan Home' (*Daily Record*, 9 September 2001); 'Depraved carer jailed forty years after abuse' (*Daily Record*, 29 September 2001); 'Children in Quarriers Home suffered seven-year sex ordeal' (*Scotsman*, 8 September 2001). The fact that Samuel McBrearty (who had gone on to become a respected senior social worker in Aberdeen after he left Quarriers) had committed his crimes forty years earlier made no difference to their wickedness and little difference to the public perception of Quarriers' present-day responsibility. As the police investigation into other allegations against former staff continued, Phil Robinson knew that Quarriers had to act decisively to deal with the crisis; so he launched a huge internal inquiry to find out what had gone wrong in the past and to ensure that proper measures were in place to prevent it happening in the future. He also set up a helpline for former Girls and Boys so that they could phone in confidence if they wanted to allege that they had been abused, or to ask for help and advice. Quarriers appointed a specialist after-care worker to assist anyone who wished to access personal files (the organisation holds records of more than 30,000 children), and to offer advice or support for anyone who might want it.

How had the abuse happened? In an interview with the *Sunday Herald* in May 2002 Phil Robinson said:

> We thought then that anyone in a position of trust with children would never do these dreadful things. It was a different era. Now we know that some people try and get access to children to abuse them.

Quarriers Homes, like other residential institutions at the time, was in many ways a closed community. Although changes were being made, the men and women who looked after children were largely untrained and there were no police and security checks of the type which are standard today across all areas where adults have care of children. As we've seen (*see* chapter 8, 'Cottage Life'), fifty years ago there were few, if any, policies and procedures to prevent a cottage-mother or -father from ill-treating children, and if excessive cruelty was kept quiet – even at a time when physical punishment was considered justifiable – then sexual abuse would have been concealed to an even greater extent: public debate about paedophiles and the sexual abuse of children is such a headline topic in modern life that it's easy to forget that, in the past, it was simply never mentioned. Even in the Homes of the 1960s and '70s, if a child were being sexually abused he or she would have been unlikely to come into contact with trained social workers and professionals who would recognise the signs. And, quite simply, in a residential children's home in the days before police checks, where men and women had twenty-four-hour charge of children who were not their own, the potential for abuse was there.

The sexual abuse of a child is an appalling crime and Quarriers has never tried to minimise its seriousness or how deeply it damaged the lives of the victims, not just as children at the time but for the rest of their lives. As Phil Robinson described it to me in a conversation in December 2004:

> Sexual abuse has particular characteristics. It can taint people's lives and destroy their whole image of themselves. It's uniquely destructive.

The fact that men and women were coming forward more than forty years later is proof of how long-term the damage can be. After the Samuel McBrearty case, charges were brought against three other former Quarriers' employees – Joseph Nicholson, John Porteous and Alexander Wilson – and convictions followed. Joseph Nicholson was jailed for two years in 2001 for abusing a thirteen-year-old girl in the late 1960s, and John Porteous (who had himself been brought up in Quarriers Homes and then became a house-father) was convicted of offences against two boys between 1969 and 1976. He was jailed in November 2002 for eight years (later reduced to five). His brother-in-law, Alexander Wilson, also a former house-parent, was sent to prison in 2004 for seven and a half years for sexual abuse.

Quarriers has not been alone as an organisation in having to face up to the issue of historic child abuse. In December 2004 Jack McConnell, the First Minister of the Scottish government, issued an apology 'on behalf of the people of Scotland' to victims of institutional sexual abuse in the past. It came during a debate on a petition brought to Parliament by Chris Daly, who claims that he was abused as a child in Nazareth House, a Roman Catholic children's home in Aberdeen. His petition was lodged at a time when other cases of historic child abuse in several institutions in Scotland were coming to light, including Nazareth House, and a List D school near Stirling. The petition called for:

> ... the Scottish Executive to conduct an inquiry into past institutional child abuse, particularly for those children who were in the care of the state under supervision of religious orders, to make an unreserved apology for said state bodies, and to urge the religious orders to apologise unconditionally.[*]

In 2004 Phil Robinson gave written evidence to the Public Petitions Committee in which he pointed out, for the record, that Quarriers did not fall, and had never fallen, into the category of a religious order taking care of children on behalf of the State. He went on:

> Quarriers today is a very different organisation from that which once existed. It is no longer involved in mainstream residential childcare and most of its services are based at more than one hundred locations throughout Scotland and beyond, rather than at Quarriers Village, as was the case prior to 1980. Since the issue of abuse first arose we have been proactive in implementing child protection policies and procedures which compare well with those of any other agencies and offer the best possible protection for children involved in our services. We are not complacent, however, and are constantly open to advice as to how those policies and procedures can be improved ... I and other senior managers at Quarriers stand ready to meet and discuss issues relevant to past child abuse, whenever this is helpful. In no way does Quarriers seek to cover up or evade the consequences of these events ...
>
> As I am sure the Committee is aware, a number of historic abuse cases have resulted in criminal convictions against former employees of Quarriers. Throughout the past four years I have consistently and publicly stated that our sympathies are with those whose lives have been blighted by the actions of those convicted individuals and that the organisation sincerely regrets these events of the past.
>
> I have met many survivors of child sexual abuse and organisations representing them. We have been more than willing to hear from their experience what more they think we can do for survivors today ... Quarriers' position is that if any individual suffered abuse at Quarriers then we apologise.

---

[*] Public Petition PE535, lodged by Chris Daly on 20 August 2002

The very least that survivors of abuse are seeking is an acknowledgement of the suffering they endured as children and the awful scars which have remained with them ever since. The present Quarriers' management was not in charge in the 1960s and '70s when those who have been convicted of abuse were working in the Village, but that does not absolve the modern organisation of its moral duty to acknowledge that crimes took place and to apologise to those who suffered abuse. Quarriers has not tried to evade that responsibility. It has sincerely tried to act in a responsible and practically helpful way throughout these events. The organisation has made much of the fact that things are very different today in terms of how staff are recruited, how they're trained and the fact that everyone is police-checked. It has also been honest enough to say that there cannot be a 100 per cent guarantee that someone who wants to abuse children in the future will not find a way to do so.

Quarriers recognises that it has a responsibility for its past, regardless of whether that past was yesterday, or fifty years ago. Phil Robinson put it to me this way:

> We have a moral responsibility to all former Boys and Girls and their descendants. We have to be there for them, and in practical terms that means preserving the records, making the records as accessible as they can be, providing support for those accessing their records . . . We have a moral obligation to do that. We also have a moral obligation with regard to other aspects of the history or heritage, to preserve it, and make sure it's here for people to know what happened here, good and bad, and a whole range of things like that. We have to do that, and to pay for the cost of it. We have that moral duty.

The organisation will have to be prepared to stick to that commitment for, perhaps, many years to come. At the time of writing there is at least one other criminal case against a former employee pending, and there are civil cases now waiting in the wings – people who want to sue Quarriers for alleged historic sexual abuse. What will be the outcome of these remains to be seen, but one thing is sure: the future for Quarriers, however dynamic and committed to caring in the twenty-first century, will always be shaped by its past – good or bad.

Chapter 16

Roots

There is another part of the human drama in the long history of Quarriers which has emerged as a vibrant presence today – Canada. Between 1872 and 1938 The Orphan Homes of Scotland sent more than 7,000 children to new lives on farms and homesteads in Ontario and beyond (*see* chapter 5, 'The Golden Bridge', and chapter 6, 'The Little Emigrants'). Many other children's charities and church organisations, including Barnardo's, also sent tens of thousands of children to Canada as part of a vast programme of child migration which began in Victorian times and did not come to an end until after the Second World War. Most of the children sent to Canada from Bridge of Weir stayed on and became Canadian citizens; they built lives for themselves, settled down and had families, and Quarriers reckons that about 200,000 present-day Canadians have roots which stretch back to the Village.

When William Quarrier sent children to work as farm hands in Ontario, or to be adopted by families on remote homesteads, he sincerely believed he was giving them a better chance for the future than if they had been left on the streets of Victorian Glasgow. Not all children were orphans: some had a parent or guardian who could not look after them, and William Quarrier always tried to ensure that such children were sent to Canada only with the permission of that parent or guardian. He set up the Fairknowe Receiving Home in Brockville, Ontario, and established a system to keep track of where the children

An ex-Boy from Canada, aged seventy-nine, visits his old cottage. He well remembers William Quarrier and his daughter Mary and was thrilled to retrace paths he had so often trod as a young boy (reproduced from the 1975 Annual Report)

were and to ensure they were being properly looked after. Other organisations were not so careful.

Much of the modern criticism of the child migration movement centres on the fact that thousands of children were simply lifted from the streets of Britain and exported wholesale by agencies which had no right to take them, often kept no records and, in some cases, claimed the children were orphans when in fact they were not. Even in the twentieth century, agencies were still sending boys and girls to Canada without proper records so that their descendants today are still trying to trace their own roots and their parents' or grandparents' stories. And being a 'Home Child' carried a stigma: people regarded you as little more than slave labour; you had no home, no background; you were an alien. Consequently, many men and women put their 'Home

Child' past behind them and never talked about it to their children. Frequently, the family only discovered after their parents had died, by finding an old photograph or letter. Dave Lorente founded Home Children Canada, and is a passionate advocate for the cause of Home children and their descendants:

> During my four decades of research into my father's past, once I guessed he might have been a child migrant, I wrote to all the major sending agencies asking two questions: What records do you have? Is my father among them? In 1990 I was asked to give a talk on a subject of my choice to our local heritage group. I said I might talk on Home children because no one seemed to know anything about them or want to talk about them. At that precise moment a fellow director piped up and said, 'I wasn't allowed to play with Home children when I was a child'. It was a magic moment. It was when I realised they had been stigmatised. Since I was in charge of the meeting I billed it as a reunion for Home children, their families, friends and the people they had been placed with. And to prove Home children were not ogres I asked a former child migrant (Joe) to talk on their behalf after I gave a slide-show on the history of child migration.
> 'What do you want me to say?'
> 'Tell it like it was.'
> Joe's first sentence was: 'I never celebrate my birthday. I celebrate the day I came to Canada.'
> Before we adjourned a voice from the back hollered: 'You seem to know where our records are. Will you help me find mine?' 'Sure!' I said. 'And will you help me, too?' 'I'll help anyone.' 'And whatcha gonna charge?' 'For you, I'll do it for nothing,' I replied.
> I might not have made that promise twelve years ago had I known that last year alone I'd be answering 4,418 requests for help and still have a growing backlog.[*]

The thirst for knowledge about one's roots is a powerful force in the Home children movement. Original migrants and their descendants want to understand the child migration story, to ask questions about why and when, to know who was responsible and what it was like to be a child migrant; and they want to know – is the story being told honestly and fully? These are questions which Quarriers has tried to answer for the orginal migrants from Bridge of Weir and their families. It was Dr Minto, the General Director back in the 1980s, who

---

[*] From *A Canadian Perspective on British Child Migration*, a talk given by Dave Lorente to the International Congress on Child Migration, New Orleans, USA, October 2002

began the process of connecting with Quarriers' Canadian past when he commissioned me to write *The Village* and asked specifically that the Canadian part of the story be researched and told. Many, many surviving migrants shared their experiences of being sent to remote farms in Ontario and forging new lives, and a line of communication was established between Bridge of Weir and Canada. Then, in 1996, to mark the organisation's 125th anniversary, the then Chief Executive, Gerald Lee, followed up these initial contacts and announced plans to hold a reunion in Canada.

So on the weekend of 26 October 1996, seventeen surviving Quarriers boys and girls who had made the journey to new lives in Canada in the 1920s and '30s attended the Kingston Gathering in Ontario, along with hundreds of descendants and families of original migrants. I was also there. It was a tremendous occasion, an opportunity for Quarriers to stretch hands across the ocean and make contact once again with a living part of its history. It was a weekend for listening and learning from the remaining survivors of the thousands of children who were sent overseas, and for welcoming them and their families back to 'the Quarriers family', as Gerald Lee described it. He said that the Gathering was about 'squaring the circle', acknowledging the past and accepting responsibility for the benefits and the faults of the emigration programme which William Quarrier began and which the organisation continued for nearly seventy years. He spoke of how Quarriers had lost touch with Canada after the end of the Second World War: 'This should never have happened. I assure you that we will not let this happen again.' The chairperson of the Gathering, Beth Bruder, whose mother, Catherine McCallum, went to Canada from Bridge of Weir, said that everyone was there to 'share our common heritage. We must remove the stigma that so many children felt in coming to Canada as Home children, and we must move to emphasise the positive contribution the children made to Canada.'

For two days over that weekend in Kingston more than 300 men and women whose lives had been changed forever by emigration met and talked and shared stories. Of the original seventeen emigrants, elderly men and women in their eighties and nineties, some were still strong and sprightly, others more frail and bent, but all of them, astonishingly, retained a distinctive Scottish 'burr' in their accents. However, the

Former Boys and Girls from Quarriers who went to Canada, reunited at the Kingston Gathering in Ontario in October 1996
Back row, left to right: Hugh Blair, Archibald Aitken, William Cameron, John Thomson, James Notman, Agnes Clarke.
Front row, left to right: John Wilson, Douglas Barbour, Jack Keir, Peter Graham, Elizabeth Parrot

number of original emigrants still alive in Canada today is small and dwindling, and the majority of people who attended the Gathering were first- and second-generation descendants.

All that Saturday morning they milled around, registering and receiving name-tags, peering at display boards which recounted the history of the Orphan Homes of Scotland, talking to Quarriers staff about the modern organisation and exchanging stories with other descendants. They had photograph albums under their arms and hand-written pages of family history in their bags and by mid-morning they were gathered in animated groups, poring over faded photographs of the young faces of their mothers, fathers, grandparents, uncles and aunts who had been sent out from Scotland.

It was a morning of discovery. Quarriers staff sat in a corner room with laptop computers, calling up records and information for the patient queue of people who were there to fill in the gaps in their family history. All morning they queued, for hours. Each person brought with them a name, and perhaps a date, and wanted to know: was my father from the Orphan Homes of Scotland? When was my mother born? Where was my grandfather born? Why was he brought up at Bridge of Weir? There were other conversations of discovery as people talked to one another and exchanged stories and found memories in common. And there was even a moment of discovery for the Mayor of Kingston, Gary Bennett, who found out, at the dinner hosted by Quarriers in the evening, that he was himself a grandson of a Quarriers boy.

The Kingston weekend began the process of rebuilding the bridge of communication and information which had been broken when the emigration programme ceased. There are thousands of Canadian men and women desperate to find out as much as they can about the lives of their ancestors who came to Canada, about why they were sent in the first place, what kinds of places they worked in, what life in Quarriers was like and whether they have family still in Scotland. 'My mother never talked much about the Home and coming to Canada,' said one woman at the Gathering, 'and I guess when I was growing up I wasn't curious enough to ask more. Then suddenly she was gone and it was too late. Now I just want to find out about her life.'

Melba Barker, whose father, William Hogarth, went to Canada in 1911, said she had come to the Gathering 'to honour my father'. Ken

McEwan's mother, Margaret McCall, was only ten when she arrived on an Ontario farm in 1910 and because she talked about it so little, he has spent years trying to find out more about her life in Scotland and in Canada; he describes those Quarriers boys and girls as 'quietly resolute people' who had so much to contend with in Canada that they 'insulated themselves from life'. He came to the Gathering to tell other descendants about his mother, to exchange feelings and thoughts about trying to piece together the missing parts of her life, and to get as much information and help from Quarriers as he could about the emigration programme.

There were many, many others like Ken McEwan and Melba Barker at the Gathering, and such was the groundswell of feeling that this time of meeting and sharing should be built upon, that the Quarriers Canadian Family was subsequently formed. The association produces a quarterly newsletter with regular updates about Quarriers work and developments within the Village, articles about Quarriers migrants, information about how to get family records from Quarriers, and more general advice about genealogical research. Kingston was the start of a real commitment on both sides of the Atlantic to keep in touch and, after that first Gathering, three more reunions were held in 1998, 2001 and 2003.

However, it was to the handful of original emigrants that the weekend of that first Kingston Gathering of 1996 really belonged. They told their stories to an audience thirsty to hear. It was a weekend of emotion and excitement generated by the potency of memory, a weekend where people listened with their hearts and imaginations. There were tears in the audience as the original emigrants sang songs they remembered from the Orphan Homes, songs they had not sung for more than sixty years yet which they sang together with flushed faces and bright eyes, as if the years in between had never happened. Peter Graham, who went to Canada in 1931 (and who died in 2002) led the company in a verse from the hymn which was sung by the children at Bridge of Weir as each party left for Canada:

Don't forget the Orphan Homes of Scotland,
Don't forget the dear friends here;
Don't forget that Jesus Christ your Saviour
Goes with thee to Canada;

And remember we are still a-praying
That your life will be good and true,
And that you may find a blessing
In the land you're going to.

Sixty-five years and a lifetime later – and Peter was still word perfect.

The wheel came round full circle a year later when, in October 1997, a party of around fifty Canadians came over to Scotland and visited Quarriers Village. Most were first-, second- and even third-generation descendants of the children who went to Canada from the Village all those years ago. For many, it was their first opportunity to see for themselves where their parents, grandparents, aunts and uncles had lived before going to Canada. However, the 'stars' of the visit were, undoubtedly, two of the original children sent to Canada: John Keir, who had left the Orphan Homes in 1927, and Peter Graham, who made the Kingston Gathering such a memorable occasion. John and Peter both lived in the Kingston area and had been friends for more than sixty years.

It was an emotional but also a happy occasion. The Canadians visited some of the original children's cottages where their ancestors had stayed and were able to fill in important gaps in their family histories and Scottish origins. On the Sunday morning a special memorial service was held in Mount Zion Church and more than a few tears were shed as the vast nave resounded once more to the tunes which hundreds of children used to sing so long ago. At the end of the service Peter Graham and John Keir were escorted out as the congregation sang 'God Be With You Till We Meet Again', the same hymn that Peter had sung at the Gathering in Kingston a year before.

A small part of Quarriers at Bridge of Weir is now Canada. After the church service a piece of ground was symbolically given into the care of Quarriers Canadian Family: Maple Grove, as it was named, was gifted as a site for a garden, a quiet place of remembrance and reflection, dedicated to the memory of all the 7,000 children who went from the village to Canada between 1872 and 1938. On a beautiful autumn day, the first maple trees were planted by John Keir and Peter Graham. The pipes played, 'O Canada' was sung and the new Quarriers Canadian Family flag – a large white Q superimposed on a red maple leaf – was proudly raised and fluttered gently in the breeze.

Peter Graham, a former Boy who went to Canada, planting a maple tree in Maple Grove in Quarriers Village, 1997

The children went to Canada with a trunk of clothes and a Bible; they forged lives for themselves in a foreign land, and in Kingston in October 1996 and at Quarriers Village a year later their families, their descendants and Quarriers honoured them for it – at last.

Chapter 17

The Never-ending Story

There is an intriguing term which refers to what happens to an organisation once the original inspirational force is gone: Founder Syndrome. When the motivation and vision of the founder of a business or pioneering venture are no longer there, the organisation has to forge a new ethos and find its way in a changed environment. The more charismatic and dynamic the individual behind the original idea, the more challenging it is for those who follow to maintain the momentum and keep things going in a fresh and innovative way.

William Quarrier was a one-man show with big, original ideas, who had no patience with committees or collegiate management. His passionate commitment to tackling poverty and homelessness, coupled with the sheer force of his personality, created a unique organisation which tried to give a better life to the weakest and most vulnerable people of his day. He lived in an age of philanthropists, a dynamic time of great opportunity and appalling deprivation, when individuals who were inspired by religious faith and social conscience to change the world around them for the better could go out and do it. And, in a sense, ever since William Quarrier died the recurring theme of the Quarriers story has been: where do we go from here and how do we keep faith, in a changing world, with our founding spirit and ideals?

In the 100-odd years since the founder died, Quarriers has weathered many storms: the problems caused by the institutionalisation of the Orphan Homes in the first half of the twentieth century; the pressing need to improve and professionalise the service in the 1960s and '70s; the failure to recognise the writing on the wall for residential childcare in the 1980s and the resulting financial crisis; the painful process of readjustment and modernisation in the 1990s; and the current issue of historic abuse cases. Each generation of managers and leaders has had to make difficult decisions and work out the best ways to continue and develop the caring work while changing with the times.

There has certainly been tremendous change. Quarriers today operates all over Scotland, running more than 100 projects in dozens of locations across the country. It has a turnover of approximately £33 million and currently employs around 1,700 staff. Through the dedication and hard work of all its staff over the years, the organisation survived the extremely difficult periods in the 1980s and early 1990s and is now one of the most highly respected, professional voluntary caring agencies in Scotland. There is still vital caring work happening in the Village – not least in the national Epilepsy Assessment Centre and in Countryview, the specialist short-break unit for children with learning difficulties. But most Quarriers projects are to be found in towns and local communities further afield: for example, Seafield School in Ardrossan, a residential school for boys and girls with social, emotional and behavioural difficulties; Larkfield Family Centre in Greenock; the Fred Martin Project (in Bearsden, Maryhill and Jordanhill in Glasgow) which supports adults with learning difficulties; and QUEST (Quarriers Education Support Team), a unique project in East Renfrewshire which helps children with special educational needs towards re-integration into the school system.

Quarriers also works overseas. With grant funding from the National Lotteries Charities Board it developed a new project in Russia in the mid-1990s, working with a small voluntary group, the Taganka Children's Fund, which was trying to support destitute families in one of Moscow's housing estates. Thousands of families live crowded together in high-rise blocks and in such dire poverty that many children lack adequate food and clothing. The Taganka Family Centre provides practical help to single-parent families who exist on incomes as low as £20 per month.

The vast bulk of Quarriers' funding comes from local authorities, through the contracts to run services. This is how modern voluntary

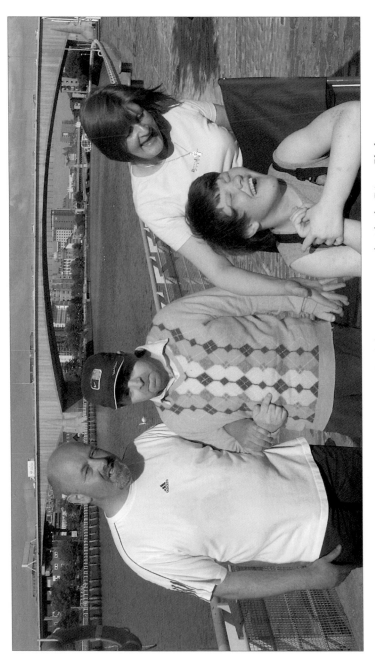

Staff and adults from Mavisbank adult respite care unit beside the River Clyde

Mavisbank adult respite care unit in Glasgow

organisations operate. A significant amount of money still comes, however, from the Scottish public, in the form of donations, fund-raising and legacies – in 2003/04 alone it totalled some £2 million. For many years Quarriers used that voluntary income to subsidise services which were not properly funded from statutory income, and a proportion of today's charitable giving is still needed to underpin existing services.

This is not ideal: Quarriers would prefer to use its voluntary income in a more imaginative and proactive way and in the late 1990s it funded several innovative projects out of a combination of 'seed money' from voluntary income and matched Lottery funding. These projects were not commissioned by local authorities, but were born out of Quarriers' own experience of needs which were not being met. Examples were the North Argyll Mobile Resource, a community development project in a remote rural area; a Befriending Service for young homeless people; and the Employment Development Initiative, which offered intensive coaching to help young homeless people into jobs or vocational training courses.

These projects were important ones which directly addressed needs which Quarriers had identified, but the problem was sustainability. The plan was that, once Quarriers had demonstrated the need and an effective means of addressing it, it would then persuade public bodies to come forward with long-term funding. This strategy failed and several of the projects had to close. Quarriers decided that funding whole projects from voluntary income in this way was not feasible, and now the practice is to contribute in smaller ways, such as funding an individual post.

The question still remains, though, and it is one which Gerald Lee, the former Chief Executive, addressed in his *Draft Strategic Plan* of 1995: what does the modern Quarriers do which reflects the innovation and originality of the organisation's founding spirit?

When William Quarrier founded the Orphan Homes of Scotland some 125 years ago, he did so because no other body, including the state, was adequately caring for the orphans and homeless children he eventually brought to Quarriers Village. Thus, in so doing, he created a service where none previously existed; he provided a solution; he plugged the proverbial gap. Above all, he acted independently . . .

It is acknowledged that the vast majority of Quarriers' operation will quite appropriately be at the behest of various local authorities. Quarriers will engage with this work in a professional and imaginative manner. However ... it is also essential that Quarriers works hard to maintain public confidence in charities in general and Quarriers in particular. An agenda for truly independent action, however limited, will capture the public imagination and promote continued support.

Phil Robinson, the present Chief Executive, believes that the future for 'truly independent action' lies not in funding innovative projects from voluntary income but in *ideas*: he wants Quarriers to be 'an influencer in society'. This is how he described his approach to me during a conversation in 2004:

We want to become an influencer in society – not in terms of becoming political or becoming a campaigning organisation but more in terms of the issues which arise from our care services: we need to be more effective in promoting these issues, making people aware of them, promoting potential solutions and improvements within society generally . . . (for example) the ways in which vulnerable adults are recognised and how they're protected within society; the Adults with Incapacity Act and the financial impact which that has on people with disabilities; child protection – who better than Quarriers to speak on that, and how that can be developed to make children safer in the future?

To this end Quarriers has recently created the post of Policy Officer and funded it entirely from voluntary income. The Policy Officer will research policy issues, help frame responses to consultations and brief managers and professionals like Phil. Most importantly, the job will involve contributing to, and influencing, the public debate on issues such as disability, care in the community, youth homelessness – all the areas where Quarriers has experience and expertise. Speaking out on important issues of the day reconnects Quarriers in a powerful way with its roots. William Quarrier wrote indignant letters to the newspapers about the scandal of street children and publicly condemned the way society treated its orphans: he spoke out powerfully against the injustices of his day, and acted positively to combat them. In a different world, modern Quarriers is trying to do the same.

It is, of course, possible to overdo the heritage and legacy thing. Quarriers is, basically, a completely different organisation, nearly a century and a half removed from its original incarnation and operating in a transformed world. But – and it is an important but – it is still primarily dedicated to helping people and caring for them; it has had a profound effect on so many thousands of lives in Scotland and beyond, and these lives connected with and gave birth to other lives, and the ripples spread outwards. So Canada is not just 'a project' in the history of Quarriers: it is about real lives and families and the good and harm which befell them as a result of their connection with Quarriers; and the criminal historic abuse cases show that when Quarriers got their care – their 'job' – wrong, it damaged real lives in a profound way, and cannot simply be consigned to history: the effects are still being felt.

Like it or not, Quarriers present is part of Quarriers past. As the story continues to unfold, more aspects of the past will emerge and be better understood in the light of experience. For instance, there is the story of the Quarriers boys and girls who went to Australia. Although some of these children have now, as adults, got back in touch with Quarriers there are still, surely, many untold stories out there. After the Canadian programme ceased, a party of thirteen boys and four girls from Bridge of Weir was sent to the Burnside Home in New South Wales in April 1939. The *Narrative of Facts* for that month has a photograph of the group on arrival in Australia, all dressed in their school uniforms, the boys in shorts and caps, the girls with hats, all looking rather shy but excited. There is no note of their ages, though they all look young, and the entry reads simply:

> The 5th day of April found us bidding farewell to thirteen of our boys and four of our girls who left us for Burnside Presbyterian Homes, Parramatta, Australia, where a warm welcome and an assured future awaited them.

Twenty years later, in January 1960, eleven boys went out to Victoria, to the Dhurringle Rural Training Farm run by the Presbyterian Church of Victoria. The *Narrative of Facts* has a little more detail this time:

> They have settled down well in their new life. Recently we received a most encouraging report from Mrs McPherson of the WVS, who was visiting in that area. They had formed themselves into a cricket team called the 'Quarrier's Warriors' and were ready to take on all comers. Australia is a land of opportunity for the young and we are certain that these new ambassadors from here will do as well as so many of our children have done in Canada.

It's a glimpse into another room of history, another story which is part of the Quarriers story, but it's indistinct and sketchy. Another ten boys went out to Dhurringle over the next two years, but there are few details in the *Narrative of Facts*. Some emigrants have told the story of what happened to them in Australia, but there are others as yet unchronicled: how did Quarriers shape their lives? When and where will their stories surface in the years to come?

On the front of the Annual Review for 2003/04 there is a picture of a busy street, with hundreds of people milling and walking about. Across it are written the words: 'Quarriers touches so many lives'. Just how many lives have been touched over the last 135 years is impossible to calculate; how many more lives in the future? As in all the best stories, it will depend on what happens next – and that chapter of *The Quarriers Story* has yet to be written.

Bibliography

The Life Story of William Quarrier, John Urquhart (R.L. Allan & Son, 1901)
A Romance of Faith, Alexander Gammie (Pickering & Inglis, 1937)
The Power I Pledge, James Ross (University Press, Glasgow, 1971)

THE NINETEENTH CENTURY
Glasgow: The Making of a City, Andrew Gibb (Croom Helm, 1983)
The New Statistical Account of Lanarkshire 1841 (William Blackwood & Sons)
The Former and Present State of Glasgow, James Clelland (Bell & Bain, 1837)
Maintenance of the Poor, James Clelland (Glasgow, 1828)
Pictures of Pauperism, ed. Donald Ross (George Gallie, 1847)
The Dawn of Scottish Social Welfare: A Survey from Medieval Times to 1863, Thomas Ferguson (Thomas Nelson & Sons Ltd, 1945)
The Children's Labour Question: Reprints from the Daily News (1899)
This is Your Child: The Story of the NSPCC, Anne Allan and Arthur Morton (Routledge, Keegan & Paul, 1961)
Annual Reports of the Glasgow Society for the Prevention of Cruelty to Children 1885–1889
Barnardo, Gilliam Wagner (Eyre & Spottiswoode, 1979)
The Life of George Müller, William Henry Hardy (Morgan & Scott, 1914)
Memoirs of the Late Dr Barnardo, Mrs Barnardo and James Marchant (Hodder & Stoughton, 1907)
The Health of Glasgow 1818–1925, A.K. Chalmers (Bell & Bain, 1930)

CANADA
Canadians in the Making, A. Lowe (Longman, Canada, 1958)
The Little Immigrants, Kenneth Bagnell (Macmillan of Canada, 1980)
British Children in Canadian Homes, Ellen Agnes Bilbrough (Houghton & Co., London, 1879)

BIBLIOGRAPHY

EPILEPSY

Epilepsy Explained, M.V. Laidlaw and John Laidlaw (Churchill Livingstone, 1980)
A Textbook of Epilepsy, ed. Laidlaw and Riches, chapter 15 (Churchill Livingstone, 1982, 2nd revised edition)

THE TWENTIETH CENTURY

The Third Statistical Account of Scotland, Glasgow Volume (Collins, 1958)
Children in Care: The Development of the Service for the Deprived Child, Jean S. Heywood (1978 revised edition)
The Child's Generation: Childcare Policy in Britain, Jean Packman (Basil Blackwell & Martin Robertson, 1981 revised edition)

PAPERS, REPORTS ETC

The Administration of Children's Homes (Scotland) Regulations 1963 (HMSO)
Staffing of Local Authority Children's Departments, report by the Scottish Advisory Council on Childcare 1963 (HMSO)
The Childcare Service at Work, report by the Scottish Advisory Council on Childcare 1963 (HMSO)
Childcare 1966, report by the Secretary of State for Scotland (HMSO)
Whose Children? letter from Marjory Allen of Hurtwood to *The Times*, 15 July 1944
The Clyde Report, 1946
Room to Grow, report of a Regional Council officer/member working group on childcare services in Strathclyde (1978)
Home or Away? report by the Director on residential childcare (Strathclyde Regional Council Social Work Department, 1983)
Caring for People (HMSO, 1990)

MANUSCRIPTS, ANNUAL REPORTS

Diaries of Admission 1890–1891 (Quarrier's Archives)
Narratives of Facts 1872–1983 (Quarrier's Archives)

Index

INDEX